Contents

Introduction

When we think of accidents, we sometimes think of Laurel and Hardy merrily hitting each other in the head with swinging ladders while cans spill paint all over their clothes.

While this may be funny in the movies, there's not much to laugh about when accidents occur in real life. Accident statistics are staggering:

- Every six minutes an American dies as a result of an accident.
- Every four seconds someone is seriously injured in an accident.
- Accidents are the fourth leading cause of death in the United States (behind heart disease, cancer, and stroke) and the leading cause of death among people age one to thirty-seven years old.
- Every year, accidents cost the United States a total of $177.2 billion in lost wages and work, property damage, insurance administration, and medical expenses.

And the list goes on and on.

This book will show you how to prevent the most common accidents in your home, on the job, and while you travel. It will show you how to keep your children safe at school and in the playground. You'll learn how to thwart life-threatening accidents on the road, on the water, and in the air. You'll learn how not to be a victim of violent crime and how to choose the safest baby products.

You won't find long-winded treatises on health and safety here. Instead, this book is packed with easy-to-use, practical advice. You'll get the most important and most useful information quickly in a fast-read format that is simple to digest and understand. You can put this information to use immediately when the need arises.

One of the special features of this book is "Safety by the Numbers." These bite-sized pieces of information, scattered throughout the book, make interesting dinner conversation, but they're much more than that. They alert you to common but crucial safety situations that you may not have thought about before. For example, "The leading cause of work injury is from overexertion," and "More than 200,000 injuries are sustained every year on playground equipment." By giving you actual statistics (many of them rather amazing and frightening), "Safety by the Numbers" calls your attention to situations and conditions that will spur you to act more safely.

As you read through this book, you may come across statistics that are a year or two old, but rest assured that these are the most up-to-date statistics available. Not only does it take time to compile the raw data, but some surveys are not done annually because of the sheer volume of work involved.

Many people have helped on this project, and I would like to acknowledge some of them: Joan DeVasty, industrial hygienist in the Environment, Safety, and Health Division of the Princeton University Plasma Physics Laboratory; Dan Fisher, staff review officer in the Palm Bay, Florida, Police Department Office of Professional Standards; Robert Gardner, principal consultant and owner of Protection Concepts in Ventura, California; Tom Pohlman, environmental health specialist in the East Carolina University Department of Environmental Health and Safety; and Peter Zavon, senior industrial hygienist with Xerox Corporation.

I would also like to thank the many people, too numerous to mention, who helped supply the latest information and statistics about accidents and accident prevention from these federal agencies: Bureau of Justice Statistics, U. S. Coast Guard, Consumer Product Safety Commission, U. S. Department of Agriculture, U. S. Department of Labor, Environmental Protection Agency, National Highway Traffic Safety

Administration, National Institute for Occupational Safety and Health, National Oceanic and Atmospheric Administration, Occupational Safety and Health Administration, and the U. S. Food and Drug Administration. I would also like to thank the American Red Cross, as well as the National Safety Council, which has perhaps the most comprehensive information about accidents of any private organization. *Accident Facts,* published annually by NSC, may be the finest compilation of accident statistics anywhere. Unless otherwise noted, all statistics in this book are derived from National Safety Council data.

It should also be noted while every effort has been made to present the most accurate safety information and advice available, the best experts often disagree. When I could not find a clear consensus, I included differing viewpoints, all of which may be valid depending upon individual circumstances.

The goal of this book is rather lofty: to keep your life and the lives of your family members as accident-free as possible. That's my goal. If something you learn here prevents an accident or saves you from harm, or if you would like to communicate with me directly, please write to me at P.O. Box 2732, Alexandria, Virginia 22301.

Think safety!

Ken Lawrence
August 1993
Washington, D.C.

CHAPTER

Home Safe Home

HOME SWEET HOME.

Yes, but is it home *safe* home as well? It could be, but statistics to the contrary are alarming. According to the National Safety Council almost twenty-one thousand people died in household accidents in 1991. In addition, more than three million people were injured in accidents in the home.

Ironically, most of these accidents are preventable. No one, of course, can ever ensure you that you will never have a mishap, but with some careful preparation you can cut down your chances of having an accident. Moreover, if an accident should happen, planning and training can increase your chances that it will be minor instead of fatal.

Falls

The most common type of home injury is the result of falling, sometimes simply (and often embarrassingly) tripping. More than six thousand people died from home falls in 1991.

As you might expect, most of the major injuries from falls are to elderly people, those sixty-five years old and older, who often have poor vision, hearing, and balance. Many older people also take medicines that can cause dizziness or tiredness. Sadly, oldsters have frailer bones that can break more easily than those of younger people. In addition, they have less muscle tension and strength to keep their joints from bending the wrong way.

And although parents of a soon-to-be-walker will tell you that their child falls constantly in his or her quest for toddlerdom, those falls don't seem to cause major injuries. Usually bruises, bumps, and split lips top the list of infants' fall-related injuries, but children this age heal rather quickly. Another reason why infants seem to make it through this unbalanced and topsy-turvy time despite all the falls is that parents are very aware of their child's interest in walking, and they keep a close eye on him or her. The common practice of childproofing one's home also keeps down the number of injuries to children. The moral of this story is that thinking about safety pays dividends.

Even so, more children under age two years die of injuries from accidents than any other cause. (Chapter 8 is devoted to baby and child safety, so we won't dwell on it here. However, we will discuss some accident-prevention issues as they pertain to babies in this and following chapters as they arise.)

Falls occur in all areas of the house, but as you accident-proof your home, pay particular attention to the stairs, bathroom, and kitchen.

Stairs

The first place to check for safety is the stairs. They should be well lighted so that each step, especially the step edges, can be clearly seen while you go up and down them. The lighting should not produce glare or shadows along the stairway.

If increased lighting is necessary, use the maximum wattage bulb allowed by the light fixture. (But if the fixture label doesn't have a maximum wattage, use a bulb no larger than sixty watts to prevent a fire hazard brought on by too much heat.) Have a qualified electrician add additional light fixtures if you need them. Reduce glare by using frosted bulbs, indirect lighting, shades, or globes on light fixtures. Partially close blinds and curtains if sunlight streams in and causes a glare on the stairs.

If you don't already have them, consider installing light switches at the top and bottom of the stairs that allow you to turn the light on and off from either place. If this isn't possible, consider using night-lights at nearby outlets.

SAFETY BY THE NUMBERS

Almost 1.5 million injuries were associated with stairs, ramps, landings, and floors in the United States in 1989.

Check the stair handrails. Repair any breaks or any part of the handrail that is not smooth to the touch. Handrails should provide a comfortable grip so you are not reluctant to use them whenever you are climbing up or going down. Use the handrail every time!

Make sure the fixtures supporting the handrail to the wall are tight and secure. Sometimes all it takes is a few turns of a screwdriver to fix a wobbly handrail. If your stairs don't have any handrails, you should install at least one on the right side as you face down the stairs.

Accidents have occurred when people have misjudged the length of the stairs because a short handrail doesn't extend the full length of the stairs. When the handrail ends, climbers or descenders may think they've come to the last step but they haven't. Ideally, you should replace a too-short handrail with a longer one. A similar problem can occur if the handrail is too long and extends beyond the first step.

The condition of the stairs themselves is especially important. Worn treads or loose carpeting can lead to insecure footing and falls. Make sure carpeting is firmly attached to the stairs. Try to avoid wearing smooth-soled slippers or shoes, and don't wear socks without shoes. Check the carpeting for exposed nails or tacks; if they snag your foot, you may trip.

Apply specially made, rough-textured strips to outdoor

steps. These strips are usually black and are embedded with abrasive material. Alternatively, you can coat outside steps with paint mixed with rough-textured particles resembling sand. Painting the edge of the steps white will help you see them better.

Watch out for even small differences in step heights; these can be dangerous. Mark any steps that are higher or lower than the others, and be careful when you use them.

And last but certainly not least, keep all stairs clear of toys and other debris. Objects left on stairs are a major cause of accidents.

Bathrooms

Wet, soapy surfaces—especially porcelain surfaces—are slippery and may contribute to falls. Apply textured strips or appliques to the floors of tubs and showers and use nonskid mats in the tub or shower and on the bathroom floor. If you are unsteady on your feet, use a stool with nonskid tips as a seat while showering.

Grab bars can help you get into and out of your tub or shower. Make sure they are attached to structural supports in the wall. Or you can buy bars designed to attach to the sides of the bathtub.

Kitchens

One of the main causes of falls in the kitchen is from standing on chairs or other makeshift platforms to reach high shelves. Never stand on a chair to reach something in a high cabinet or shelf. If you have a step stool, use it; if you don't, consider buying one. Choose one that has a handrail you can hold on to while standing on the top step. Make sure it has rubber-tipped legs and is sturdily built. Be certain to keep all screws and braces tightly fastened.

While step stools will lessen your chances of falling during your daily chores, they can also be dangerous if not used correctly. **Make sure the step stool is fully opened, locked, and stable before you climb on it.**

Kitchens also have other unique hazards that can cause

falls. One of them is the kitchen floor, which is subject to spills from grease, oils, and other highly slippery substances. Be sure to wipe all spills immediately.

Other Rooms

While stairs, bathrooms, and kitchens pose the greatest danger from falling, other rooms should be checked for dangerous conditions as well.

In the **living room** or **family room,** check all rugs and carpet runners for bumps, holes, and loose or frayed ends. Make certain that electrical cords and telephone wires are safely out of the way, but do not run these cords under rugs as they could cause a fire if they become frayed. Check passageways and halls for proper lighting.

In the **garage, work room,** or **basement** be careful of wet spots. Garages and carports are notorious for having oil and grease spots from cars, lawn mowers, and other engines. Clean these areas with sawdust or special grease-removing cleaners to ensure your safety and that of your family.

Ladders

Ladders are dangerous tools and deserve respect. Your first step (no pun intended) is to make sure the ladder you are using is safe. A high-quality ladder will be strong and sturdy with no loose steps or missing rungs.

When using a folding stepladder, make sure it is fully opened and that the paint-holder platform is in its proper position. Never use a stepladder that leans against a wall. Instead, open it fully and position it next to the wall. Pay heed to the following piece of advice you will see, in various wordings, on every folding stepladder:

Do not stand on the top step.

Standing on the top step of a ladder is dangerous because you are in an unstable position. When you're standing on one of the lower rungs, you can stabilize yourself by pressing your legs or shins against the rung above. When you're on the top step, you have no such security. On some stepladders the next-to-the-top rung is also marked as "no-step." Heed that advice.

Never have more than one person on a stepladder unless it's specifically labeled a "two-person" ladder, and never step on the bracing rungs on the "back" side. They are designed for exactly that—bracing—and not for stepping.

When using an extension ladder, a good rule of thumb is that the ladder should be about three to four feet longer than the height you want to reach. For example, if you are trying to reach a roof the ladder should extend about three feet above the roof so you can grasp the ladder's side rails when getting on and off the roof. It can be dangerous to stand on the last three rungs of an extension ladder; you will not be adequately balanced and you could slip.

Now is a good time to discuss how you climb or descend a ladder. Did you ever see fire fighters climb a ladder? They grasp the sides of the ladder, not the rungs. It's the safest method.

Make sure your ladder is firmly secured on the ground. If the terrain is mushy you should place a piece of wood underneath the legs of the ladder to keep it from sinking. If the ground is covered with loose rocks, you might place a wide plank underneath the legs to keep the ladder from sliding.

Carrying items such as paint cans up a ladder is tricky and can be dangerous. The safest method is to carry a rope with a hook as you climb the ladder, then lower the hook to a buddy who can attach the paint can for you to lift once you're in place. That buddy should also be watching the ladder's legs for any sign of slippage or movement. The safest way is to tie the ladder to an immovable object (the house or a fence) if possible.

One last piece of advice on ladders: *Never exceed the maximum load weight.* Each ladder will have a label giving the maximum load it can hold. Do not go over that weight.

When working on electrical projects or near power

lines, be very careful where you place your ladder. If possible, use a wooden or fiberglass ladder when working near power lines because metal ladders conduct electricity very well and could be dangerous. Wood or fiberglass is less prone to conduct electricity but can conduct high currents if wet.

Ice and Snow

Nearly half of all falls on ice result in broken bones. The best advice is not to walk on ice patches at all. Walk around them if possible.

Clear snow from well-traveled areas such as sidewalks and steps before the snow gets trampled and packed into ice. Sprinkle an abrasive such as sand on any areas you can't clear. Ice melters such as salt, calcium chloride, and other chemicals melt the ice unless the temperature is too low. Check the label instructions before you spread them. If the temperature is too low, you're just wasting your money and time.

If you must walk on icy surfaces, do it the safest way: lean forward as you walk. Take small steps and bend your knees. If you must carry items like books or groceries, use a backpack. This will keep your hands free for balance and to help break your fall if you go down. Never put your hands in your pockets when you're walking on ice. Be sure to wear gloves or mittens. They not only keep your hands warm, they also prevent cuts and scrapes if you fall.

If you are agile enough to do so (and not too startled by the experience!), try to go limp and roll as you land from a fall.

Here's one other common-sense piece of advice: be mindful that while the sun is shining, the snow may melt and be less slippery, but when nighttime comes and temperatures drop, packed snow can quickly turn to hard, slippery ice.

Fire Safety

Since humankind's earliest days, fire has been an indispensable part of our lives. It keeps us warm, cooks our food, and helps produce power for industry and manufacturing.

Since those earliest days, fire has also been our enemy. Fire and smoke are the third leading cause of accidental deaths in the home. In fact, the United States has the highest per capita death rate from fires of any industrialized nation.

The property costs of fire losses are staggering as well. Each year, more than $7 billion are lost because of fire.

While fire itself is a rather complex chain of chemical reactions, only three items are necessary for fire to occur. These items comprise what is called the *fire triangle*. If just one of these components is missing, fire will not happen:

Fuel: A fire's fuel can be solid, such as furniture or rugs, or liquid, such as gasoline or kerosene. Fuel can also be gas, such as propane.

Heat: For a fire to start the fuel must be hot enough to reach its *kindling temperature,* the temperature at which it will actually burn. Some solids, such as newspaper, have a relatively low kindling temperature while some woods, especially thick pieces, have a relatively high kindling temperature. That's why many people build a fire by first igniting newspaper, then adding small twigs, then thicker pieces of wood until the flame heats a thick log hot enough to ignite and finally burn.

Oxygen: Fires consume oxygen. (The air we breathe is composed of oxygen, nitrogen, and traces of other gases.) Without oxygen fires go out very quickly. This is the secret behind the *stop-drop-and-roll* method of extinguishing flames if your clothes catch on fire.

The essence of fire fighting is to deprive the fire of at least one of these items. For example, water sprayed on a fire will cool it down, robbing it of needed heat. Forest-fire fighters use another method. You've probably heard of "fighting fire with fire." That's the idea when they intentionally burn a section of forest in front of a moving fire. By burning trees in the path of the fire, they are taking away potential fuel from the forest fire.

Heating Devices

One of the leading causes of house fires is heating devices: misused or defective space heaters, furnaces, wood-burning stoves, central heating systems, and other home heating devices, along with their ancillary components such as chimneys and flues. These devices are used the most and are at their highest level of operation during the winter. This is why most house fires occur during that season.

To protect your home and family from fire caused by these heating devices, be sure they are installed and used correctly and that they are in top condition.

Although fires sometimes occur as the result of defective central heating systems, many more fires are caused by defective or misused supplemental or portable heaters. Some of these devices also present a second danger: poisoning by noxious fumes or suffocation when the fumes replace breathable air in your house. Many such accidents can be prevented by properly installing, maintaining, and caring for portable heaters. Each device presents different problems and each must be handled individually.

Wood-Burning Stoves and Fireplaces. One of the main causes of fires from wood-burning stoves and fireplaces is poor installation. Make sure your fireplace or stove meets all fire and building codes. If you have any doubt, call the fire marshal or fire inspector for advice. Then follow these suggestions as you use your stove or fireplace:

- Always follow the label instructions for operation.
- Inspect the stove regularly (usually twice a month is sufficient) according to the manufacturer's instructions.
- Have your chimney inspected and cleaned by a professional chimney sweep to remove creosote, a natural by-product of burning wood that builds up in chimneys and can catch fire. To reduce creosote buildup, avoid smoldering fires.
- Install a noncombustible floor protector that extends at least eighteen inches beyond the fireplace or around all sides of the stove. This will cut down on the chance of a stray spark shooting out of the stove or fireplace and igniting rugs, draperies, or upholstery.
- Always use a screen that completely covers the open-

ing of a fireplace to prevent sparks from flying out
onto rugs and furniture.

- Never burn trash in a stove because this could overheat the stove. Never start a fire with gasoline or other
flammable liquids because the gasoline or other liquid
could ignite and explode.
- Use chimney guards to keep out small animals and
birds' nests.
- Never burn any material other than wood (such as
coal) unless the manufacturer says it is acceptable. If
your stove or fireplace can handle artificial logs, burn
only one at a time. Because of their sawdust and wax
content, they produce a lot of heat, and burning more
than one log at a time could produce too much heat
for the fireplace to handle.
- Always keep a tight-lidded metal container for ash removal. Never place ashes in your regular trash container.
- Make sure the fire is completely out before you go to
bed.

Kerosene Heaters. One of the biggest dangers with kerosene heaters is that the kerosene can spill if the heater is
moved. Never move the heater while it is operating. If you do
spill some kerosene, wipe it up immediately. Follow these additional recommendations as you use your heater:

- *Never* use any other liquid except kerosene in your
heater. Gasoline and other combustible liquids can explode. To reduce the risk of mistakes, keep kerosene
(and all liquids for that matter) in appropriate containers that are *clearly marked.*
- Place the heater so it will not be knocked over by people walking through the house.
- Use "1K" kerosene. Other grades of kerosene contain
much more sulfur and will increase sulfur dioxide
emissions that can be poisonous.
- Never fill the heater while it is operating. To prevent
spillage on rugs that could later ignite, always take the
heater outside to refill it.

- Kerosene heaters are not usually vented to the outside, so make sure the room is well ventilated by keeping a window or door open. Some experts say you can never truly ventilate the room adequately to accommodate a kerosene heater without opening up many windows and losing a lot of heat to the outside.
- Keep all flammable liquids such as paints away from the heater.
- If a flare-up occurs, never try to move the heater or try to smother the flames with a rug or blanket. Turn the manual shutoff switch and call the fire department. Moving the heater could cause you to spill kerosene on yourself.
- **If you buy kerosene from a gas station, make certain you are using the kerosene pump and not the gasoline pump.**

Gas-Fired Space Heaters. Vented gas-fired space heaters are safer than unvented ones. However, if you must use an unvented heater, use one that has a *pilot safety system* that turns off the gas if there is not enough fresh air available. Follow these addition recommendations when using a gas-fired space heater:

- Unvented gas heaters should never be used in small, enclosed areas, especially bedrooms. There is always a potential danger of carbon monoxide poisoning if exhaust gases cannot escape. (Later in this chapter we'll address this danger in greater detail when we discuss indoor air pollution.)
- Do not use a propane heater with a gas cylinder stored in the body of the heater or stored anywhere else in the house. This is against fire regulations in most areas of the United States.
- Follow the manufacturer's instructions for lighting the pilot light. It's always possible that gas vapors have accumulated, and these vapors will ignite explosively. To prevent gas buildup, light the match first, then turn on the gas.
- Keep all flammable materials away from the heater.

- Never operate a *vented* gas-fired heater in an *unvented* manner. Combustion materials such as carbon monoxide could build up and cause illness or death.

SAFETY BY THE NUMBERS

Accidents are the leading cause of death among people from one to thirty-seven years old. For people fifteen to twenty-four years old, accidents claim three times more lives than the next leading cause.

Portable Electric Heaters. The Consumer Product Safety Commission estimates that half of the deaths and one-third of the injuries resulting from electric heaters occur at night while families are asleep and the heaters are unattended. Although the electric heaters themselves are sometimes at fault, the problem can also be caused by an extension cord that is too small to carry the large power requirements of the heater. Follow these suggestions when using an electric heater:

- Follow the manufacturer's recommendations for placement. Usually the recommended minimum distance between the heater and upholstery, drapes, and beds is three feet.
- Using an electric heater in your bathroom is especially dangerous due to the risk of both electrocution (resulting from water on the floors and counters) and fire. **Never place electric heaters in areas where towels or other flammable items can fall on them.**
- Avoid using extension cords with heaters unless it's absolutely necessary. If you must use an extension cord, make certain it is marked with a power rating that is at least as high as the power rating of the heater. Do not place anything on the cord and do not position it under rugs or carpeting.
- Never use heaters to warm or dry clothes or shoes. Use heaters only to heat the room.
- Never place electric heaters on cabinets, chairs, or tables.

- **Always turn electric heaters off whenever the house is empty or when family members are asleep.**

Cooking Fires

Kitchens, like supplemental heat sources, are inherently dangerous because we intentionally produce fire and heat in them. And we do it often. Many kitchen fires are the result of carelessness and poor housekeeping. Whenever you cook, do not wear loose, billowy clothing that can easily fall on burners or heating elements. Pay particular attention to loose sleeves. All it takes is a quick reach over the burners.

Be very careful when you deep-fry foods. Heat the oil slowly and be aware that oil may not look hot if it isn't bubbling, but it can be very hot indeed.

Never use water to put out a grease or oil fire. Water added to a grease fire will boil, then turn to steam, which can scald you. Instead, put out grease fires by smothering them. If a fire starts in a pan, place a lid on top of it and don't open it until you are absolutely sure the fire is out. Alternatively, douse the flames with lots of baking powder or use a fire extinguisher designed for grease and oil fires.

Fires often start in ovens when you open the door to check your food, allowing oxygen to enter. If a fire starts in the oven, close the door. This will help smother the flames. Turn off the oven and wait. Don't take the food out until you are sure the flames are out. Keep your face away from the oven door, especially if it has a glass panel. Although this glass is designed to take high heat, it is not designed for sustained exposure to open flames and can crack or shatter.

For microwave-oven fires the same rules apply: close the door and keep it closed until you are absolutely sure the fire is out.

One last word on kitchen fires: **Never leave food cooking on the stove when you go out.** There is great temptation to leave foods in the oven on "low" and then go out for several hours. Don't do it. More major house fires are caused by unattended cooking than by any other reason.

■ Ranges and Ovens ■

Follow these recommendations when using your kitchen range or oven:

- Keep small children away from ranges and ovens when in use. Do not store items of interest to children above the range.
- At some heat settings, it is difficult to tell when an electric burner is on. Always check controls to make sure the heating elements are off when you have finished cooking.
- Do not use the range or oven to heat the room.
- Clean grease spots from range surfaces to minimize chances of a fire.
- Turn pot handles away from the range front (but not over the other cooking elements or burners) to reduce the possibility of burns from spilling hot food or accidentally touching hot handles.
- Do not place excessive weight on open oven doors; it could cause the oven to tip over.
- If you smell gas when using the range or oven, turn off all controls and extinguish any open flame. Open a window to ventilate the room. **Don't touch any electrical switches. Call the gas company immediately from a neighbor's phone.**
- Keep pilot lights burning at all times. If you are unsure about relighting a pilot light that has gone out, call your gas company.
- Never use flammable liquids such as gasoline, kerosene, or paint thinner around a gas range. The pilot light can ignite flammable vapors.
- If the gas flame is yellow, the burner is not adjusted properly. Call a service technician or refer to the owner's manual to adjust the burner.
- Never leave pot holders on the range top.

Flammable Liquids

Garages and storage areas can also be dangerous areas because of what is kept there. Check to make sure all flammable liquids are stored in properly labeled, tightly closed, nonglass containers. Store these products away from heat sources such as furnaces and water heaters. Whenever you use one of these products, open the can outside if possible to dissipate any fumes that may have collected in the empty portion of the container. This is especially important for containers that have only a little liquid inside and contain a very vaporous substance such as gasoline. Of course you should never open a container near a heat source. Also keep it away from electrical sparks that could ignite the vapors. Remember that electric motors, like those used in sump pumps, produce sparks.

If you smell vapors in your garage, basement, storage closet, or wherever flammable liquids are stored, do not turn on the light switch. The electrical spark could ignite the vapors. Instead, ventilate the area first, then locate the leaking container. If possible, store all flammable liquids outside your home. A shed unconnected to the house is the safest storage area.

SAFETY BY THE NUMBERS

Open wounds and lacerations are the most common injuries in the United States. Sprains and strains are second.

Smoking

Although cigarette smoking is not the leading cause of residential fires, it is the leading cause of residential fire *deaths*. Conventional wisdom tells us that smoking in bed is the culprit, but actually that is only true in part because since the mid-1970's, bedding material has been required to be fire resistant. Still, smoking in bed is very dangerous and should never be permitted.

More cigarette-related fires are actually caused by a cigarette falling between the cushions of a couch or easy chair where it may ignite the furniture and smolder, unnoticed, for hours while the family sleeps. Then, in the middle of the night, a fire ignites and the house is engulfed before anyone is aware of it.

The main cause of smoking-related fires is carelessness. While all of us are careless at one time or another, elderly people are particularly susceptible to smoking dangers. Impaired vision, poor mobility, and the effects of medications make them more prone to causing cigarette-induced fires.

If elderly people in your house smoke, make sure plenty

of oversized ashtrays are available. Ashtrays should never be placed on the arms of chairs or couches because they can easily be spilled.

Never dump ashtray debris into the regular trash; paper and other materials may catch on fire. Instead, empty ashtrays into separate, metal containers. Clean all ashtrays before you go to sleep. In fact, empty all ashtrays before you leave a room. This ritual will ensure that no smoldering cigarette butts can somehow be knocked over onto a rug or upholstery.

If you should drop a cigarette on upholstery, retrieve it immediately. Check thoroughly for any ashes or sparks behind the cushions, under pillows, and under the furniture itself. Check the surrounding rugs and draperies. If furniture does catch fire, call the fire department immediately. It is very difficult to extinguish upholstery fires on your own.

Furniture also presents other dangers when ignited. Many people die from toxic gases released by smoldering upholstery without ever smelling smoke or seeing flames. Consider fire safety before purchasing your next piece of furniture. In general, fabrics made of vinyl, wool, or those containing 50 percent polyester or more of polyolefin, nylon, acrylic, polyester, or acetate fibers can be expected to resist smoldering better than other fabrics. The resistance of cotton, rayon, or linen fabrics to smoldering cigarettes depends upon the weight of the fabric. The heavier the fabric, the less easily the fabric will catch on fire. In general, furniture manufactured within the last ten to fifteen years tend to be more fire resistant then those produced before.

Place all upholstered furniture, including beds, away from heat sources such as fireplaces, stoves, and space heaters. Check all electric cords near beds and upholstered furniture and make sure they are not frayed or defective.

Smoking dangers are not limited to cigarettes; lighters and matches present problems too. Disposable lighters are a little safer than old-fashioned lighters in that they are not refilled from cans of flammable liquid. Also, if one drops from your hand the flame goes out because your thumb must press the button to keep it lit. Older lighters continue to stay lit even if dropped.

Clothing

Although there is great emphasis on fire-resistant night-clothes for children, adults should be aware of their night clothes as well. A significant number of clothing fires occur in the over sixty-five age group, principally from nightwear such as robes, pajamas, and nightgowns. Small, open flames including matches, cigarette lighters, and candles, are the main culprits, but ranges and heaters also ignite clothing.

Always check the fiber content when purchasing clothes and look for fibers that are difficult to ignite and burn, especially cotton, rayon, and polyester that are labeled *flame resistant*. Also look at the weave; tightly woven clothes without a fuzzy or napped surface are less likely to ignite and burn than open knits and weaves or fabrics with brushed or pile surfaces.

Consider purchasing clothes that can be removed without pulling them over your head. If you should have to remove them in a hurry, easily removed clothes prevent burns.

■ Stop, Drop, and Roll ■

If your clothes catch on fire there is only one safe way to save yourself—it's the stop-drop-and-roll method:

1. Stop! Running will only fan the flames higher.
2. Drop! Drop to the ground. Cover your face with your hands.
3. Roll! Roll over and over to smother the flames.

If you buy clothing that is flame resistant, be sure to follow the label's washing instructions. Improper cleaning may strip the fabric of its flame-resistant properties.

Smoke Detectors

Smoke detectors can increase your family's chances of surviving a fire by 50 percent. It may be the single most important fire-prevention factor in your home. In many municipalities, smoke detectors are required by law. They must be built into new homes and retrofitted into existing homes that are remodeled or resold.

Buying a Smoke Detector. Smoke detectors come in two styles, based on power source. The first kind is powered by your home's electrical system. The advantage of this kind is that you never have to worry about replacing batteries. The downside is that if your power goes out, such as during a storm, you will be without protection. This is more of a danger than you might imagine because when the lights go out you are more likely to light candles or use other flames for illumination. However, you may not have a choice due to your local fire and building codes. Some require battery-operated smoke detectors while others allow a choice.

One option is to buy an AC-powered smoke detector with a battery backup. This offers maximum protection. However, it's not worth it to rewire the house just to install this type of smoke detector.

Most fire experts recommend battery-operated smoke detectors or AC-powered detectors with battery backup. Smoke-detector operation twenty-four hours a day—no matter what the status of your household AC power—is the goal.

There are also different types of smoke detectors based on how they detect fire. Far and away the most common is the *ionization* detector, which uses a minute piece of radioactive material (it's not dangerous at all; it's shielded) to produce a field of radioactive ions that allow an electrical current to flow. While that current flows, the detector is quiet. Once smoke enters the field, it disrupts the electrical flow and an alarm sounds. Ionization detectors are extremely sensitive to even the smallest smoke particles; even particles you can't see can be detected.

The other kind of smoke detector uses a *photoelectric* cell. This is very similar to the system used by some burglar alarms. A small beam of light is part of an electrical circuit. As long as the light beam stays constant, the alarms stays off. If anything—like smoke particles—breaks that beam, the alarm sounds. As you might guess, photoelectric detectors react more quickly to larger smoke particles than to small ones. Smoldering fires give off larger particles than blazing fires.

Which one should you buy? Both types have their advantages and disadvantages, but the ionization type may offer slightly more protection because it detects smaller particles than the photoelectric type. That's why they've become the most popular type.

Take Good Care of Your Smoke Detectors

Smoke detectors don't need much attention except for regular testing and prompt replacement of batteries. However, if you neglect these few requirements your detector won't do its job if a fire starts.

1. **Test** your smoke detectors periodically according to the testing procedures described in your instruction book. Usually once a month is recommended. In some very old models you must test the unit with smoke from an extinguished candle or cigarette. In newer models, pressing the "test" button will check the unit for proper functioning.
2. **Replace batteries** according to the instructions in your manual. For most detectors, at least once a year is adequate or when it makes a chirping tone indicating a low-battery level. One easy way to remember when to change batteries is to do so when you change the clocks for daylight savings time.
3. Don't play with the smoke detectors. Remind everyone in your home, especially children, that smoke detectors should not be touched or played with. **Never paint a smoke detector's casing.**
4. Don't disconnect your smoke detector if it acts erratically. Immediately replace it.
5. Don't disconnect your smoke detector if it responds to nuisance smoke such as from cooking areas or fireplaces. Either fan away the smoke or relocate the detector.

Installation

Position—where the smoke detector is installed—is another crucial factor. Local codes take precedence over anything stated here. However, in the absence of local codes or if you want to exceed local codes (a good idea since codes usually offer minimum protection) follow these recommendations:

- Place one detector on at least every floor, including the basement.
- If any family member sleeps with his or her door bedroom door closed, place a smoke detector inside the room as well.
- Follow the instruction manual that comes with your smoke detector as to exact placement, but in general, smoke detectors should be installed on the ceiling but *not in the corner where the ceiling and wall meet*. This is a *dead zone* where air doesn't circulate. Without that circulation, the detector won't be able to sense smoke coming from other parts of the room. The center of the ceiling is the best location.
- Don't place smoke detectors near air vents as dust and small particles carried by the air can clog the device. Also, the fresh air passing by the detector may keep away smoke from the rest of the room and the alarm won't be activated.
- Don't place smoke detectors near a furnace or other source of heat.
- Don't place smoke detectors against walls or ceilings that are poorly insulated because the cold or heat may form a thermal air pocket that can keep smoke away from the detector. This is not a problem in most homes but could occur in uninsulated and unheated basements or room additions.
- Don't place smoke detectors in bathrooms. The moisture in the air can set off the alarm.
- Although it seems like a good idea, don't place smoke detectors in kitchens. Smoke from cooking food will set off the alarm, and you'll be continually annoyed by its noise. Then you'll be tempted to disconnect it, and you'll lose your protection. Instead, place the smoke detector far enough outside the kitchen so cooking smoke isn't a factor. If stray smoke should activate the

alarm, do not disconnect it. Open the windows and fan the air around the smoke detector until it dissipates enough to turn off the alarm. **Remember: If you disconnect a smoke detector you may forget to turn it back on.**

What to Do If Fire Breaks Out

The three most important ways to stop fires from happening are prevention, prevention, and prevention. That's what this book is all about—keeping accidents from happening. But fires *will* occur despite your best attempts at prevention, so you should know what to do if fire breaks out in your home.

1. Don't panic. Yes, it's easy to say that now, when there's no fire, but you will increase your chances of survival if you keep a cool head.
2. Stay low. Drop to the floor while you assess the situation. Smoke rises, so by staying low your opportunity for survival is increased. Remember, not only does fire kill, but smoke kills too.
3. Remember your escape route and implement it if you can.
4. If you're in a room with the door closed, crawl to the door and feel it with your hand. If it is hot, follow suggestions 5–10, below. If it is not hot, follow suggestions 11–15.

   If the door is hot . . .
5. **Do not open it.** A hot door could mean that the fire is just outside the room. A closed door will protect you. Opening the door will bring flames into your room. In addition, it could feed the fire with fresh oxygen.
6. Seal the door cracks with anything you have. Wet towels or clothes are best, but anything else will help.
7 Crawl to a window and open it slightly from the top

and bottom. This will let in fresh air for you to breath but not enough to draw smoke into the room.

8. Escape out the window if it's safe to do so. Break the window if you have to, but only as a last resort. Be aware that the outside of the house may be on fire too, and flames could enter through the window. If you break the window rather than open it, there will be no way to keep the flames out.

9. If you can't get out the window, summon help by screaming or making noise by clanging items together. It's better to bang things together because you want to save your breath. Waving a towel or bed sheet out the window will also attract attention.

10. If you have a phone in the room, call 911 or your local fire department number. Let them know you're trapped inside the room.

If the door is not hot . . .

11. Open it slightly to look for flames or smoke.

12. If you can escape, close the door behind you. It will keep the fire from spreading.

13. Continue to crawl. Do not get up! Alert others to the fire by pounding on the wall or yelling.

14. Don't waste time looking for valuables. Get out of the house immediately and meet your family at the predetermined meeting place.

15. Call the fire department from a neighbor's house.

■ Fire Extinguishers ■

You wouldn't expect fire extinguishers to be controversial, but they are. Fire-safety experts are always concerned that someone will try to fight a fire that is too big to be put out with a fire extinguisher and waste precious time instead of calling the fire department immediately.

Fire extinguishers can save lives and property, but only under specific circumstances. They are good for small fires that are contained in a small area. A good example would be a bunch of papers on fire in a wastepaper basket. Another appropriate instance would be a small fire in the corner of a room in which no other combustibles are around.

Before you begin to fight a fire, make sure everyone has left or is leaving the area. Call the fire department or have someone else call. Keep your back to an escape route so you can still get out if the fire grows.

Make sure the fire extinguisher is rated for the type of fire you are fighting. The labels are on the extinguisher.

Type A for ordinary combustibles: wood, cloth, paper, and wood. The fire extinguisher contains water, propelled by inert gases such as carbon dioxide, that cools the fire.

Type B for flammable liquids: gasoline, oil, grease, paint, and tar. The fire extinguisher contains dry foam or dry chemicals that smother the fire. Water isn't used because of the extremely high temperatures these fires produce.

Type C for electrical equipment: wiring, fuse boxes, circuit breakers, appliances, and motors. Nonconducting chemicals or gases smother the flames without conducting the electricity.

Multipurpose fire extinguishers (labeled ABC): These extinguishers can handle all three types of fires. (There is also a Type D fire extinguisher, found only in industrial settings, that is used on combustible metals such as magnesium and sodium.)

You must know how to use the extinguisher before the fire occurs. There's no time to read the instructions once a fire happens. Also note that many small fire extinguishers only last a short time, some as little as ten seconds. Don't fight a large fire with a small fire extinguisher.

A large fire extinguisher can be very heavy, so make sure you can lift it safely. If it is the type that rolls on a dolly or hand truck, make sure you know how to move it correctly.

Check your fire extinguishers frequently for the proper charge, and service them according to the label instructions. Reusable fire extinguishers can be used more than once but must be recharged. Disposable extinguishers are good for only one application and must be discarded. They also must be discarded about ten years after their date of manufacture, even if they've never been used. The label will give you exact details.

Fires in apartment and high-rise buildings require special procedures:

1. If the fire is not in your apartment and you are not in any danger, keep your door closed and call the fire department.
2. Know the nearest emergency stairways or outside fire escapes. If the fire is on your floor but you can escape safely, do so. As you leave, close your door behind you, and close any fire doors in the hallway as well. Take your keys. If you find that you can't leave the building because you are blocked by fire, you may have to return to your apartment.
3. If the fire is not on your floor or you are not directly above it (remember, fires tend to rise) stay inside and await directions from fire fighters.
4. Activate the building's fire alarm, remembering that many building alarms are local. They are only heard in the building and do not summon the fire department.
5. Always use the stairs. **Never use the elevators.** Walk down, not up, unless you are threatened by fire and have no alternative. Hold on to the handrails tightly. Smoke may make vision impossible, and the handrail will keep you from tripping.
6. If you are trapped in your room, use the same procedures described earlier for handling the situation "if the door is hot." However, in this case it's even more important that you let fire fighters know where you are. Open a window slightly and hang a towel or some other attention-getting item to signal fire fighters. Wave if you think you'll be seen. If you can use the phone, call the fire department to let fire fighters know where you are. Do this even if you see fire trucks outside the building.

Plan Your Fire Escape

Panic is a major cause of deaths during fire. Planning an escape route and having the entire family rehearse it could mean the difference between life and death. Practice your escape plan at least once every six months.

The majority of house fires occur at night, so it is imperative that you know your way around your house in the dark. Even during the day, smoke will diminish visibility.

■ Have a Safe Holiday Season ■

Many fires occur around the Christmas and Hanukkah seasons. Follow these suggestions to make sure your holidays are safe:

For Christmas:

- Place Christmas trees away from fireplaces, radiators, and other heat sources. Trees dry out rapidly in heated rooms, creating fire hazards.
- Keep the tree stand full of water at all times. Before putting the tree in the stand, cut off about two inches of the trunk to expose fresh wood for better water absorption.
- Artificial snow can irritate your lungs if inhaled. To avoid injury, read the container label and carefully follow the directions.
- Check each light socket on your Christmas lights for frayed connections or damaged wires. Discard any damaged sockets or repair them before using.
- Never use electric lights on a metallic tree. The tree can become charged with electricity from faulty lights, and anyone touching the tree could become electrocuted. Instead, use colored spotlights above or beside the tree, never fastened to it.
- Keep bubble-lights away from children. They can tempt curious children to play with the candle-shaped glass bubblers. Not only can the glass cause cuts, but the liquid inside may be a hazardous chemical.
- Never use lighted candles on a tree. Use only noncombustible or flame-resistant trimmings.
- Wear gloves while decorating with spun-glass "angel hair" to avoid eye and skin irritation. Put it out of children's reach.
- When making paper decorations, look for materials labeled "noncombustible" or "flame-resistant."
- Remove all wrapping paper from around the tree and fireplace immediately after presents are opened.
- Avoid trimmings that resemble candy or food. A child could eat them.

For Hanukkah:

- Make sure children understand the dangers of playing with Hanukkah candles.

- Place candles in a low-traffic area to prevent accidental bumping.
- Keep candles out of reach of very young children.
- Don't leave matches around the menorah. Put them away.
- Make sure all candles are secure in their bases, and place aluminum foil or some other nonflammable material underneath the menorah in case a candle should fall over.

Start by drawing a diagram of all floors of your house showing windows and doors. Plan at least two ways to get out of each room. Try each route, checking for problems that could pop up, such as a chair that is sometimes placed away from its usual position.

Be sure all locks and windows open easily and quickly and that all family members know how to handle them. Storm windows and window locks can sometimes be tricky to open.

Make certain to include children in all fire drills. Youngsters naturally will be scared when someone screams "Fire!" or when the loud piercing sound of the smoke detector awakens them. It's a good idea to let children hear what a smoke detector sounds like during a test so they will not panic if they hear it during a fire.

Children should know what is expected of them in fire. If a child needs a small stool to help him or her climb out of a window, provide it. If the child is unable to open a window or does not have the maturity to understand the escape route plan, he or she should learn to wait in a designated area, by a window for example, for rescue.

Also have a plan for helping elderly or handicapped people to escape and getting pets out if possible.

If you must escape from a second-story window, make sure there is a way to get down to the ground. An emergency ladder made of metal chains could work well here. Practice how to deploy and climb down.

Establish a meeting place outside the house where family members will meet after their escape. This will prevent unnecessary worrying and keep people from going back in the house to save someone who is already outside. **Once you are outside, never return inside.**

Electricity

Until 1975 more than a thousand people each year died from electrical hazards in the home, but that number has been steadily dropping. The all-time low was 714 in 1988, and there is every reason to believe that the number of deaths by electrocution will continue to drop. (These figures are for deaths directly due to electricity. It doesn't include electricity-related fires or job-related deaths caused by electricity.)

One reason for the drop in electricity-related deaths is the National Electrical Code that since 1973 has required *ground-fault circuit interrupters (GFCIs)* in newly constructed homes. Another reason is the modification of certain citizens band radio antennas, mandated by the Consumer Product Safety Commission (CPSC), which reduces consumer exposure to deadly shock should the antenna contact overhead wires. In addition, many manufacturers of electrical appliances have voluntarily provided double insulation in various power hand tools.

Based on CPSC studies, the highest rate of electrical fires occurs in houses over forty years old because of aging appliances, degradation of wiring, and the lack of GFCIs. These situations can also cause electrical shock or electrocution as well as fires. About 70 percent of U.S. households do not have GFCI protection.

Before we go any farther, let's talk about GFCIs. Without a doubt, this the single most important addition to your home that can save you from electrical shock, electrocution, and electrical fires. Simply stated, a GFCI is a switch that constantly monitors electricity flowing in the circuit. If it senses any loss of current, even a minute amount, it quickly disconnects the power to the circuit. This loss of current could be the result of a short circuit or grounding of the circuit such as when a hair dryer is dropped into the bathtub or when you

■ Extension Cords ■

Many accidents occur due to defective or improperly used extension cords. Follow these suggestions for using extension cords safely:

- Use extension cords only when necessary.
- Use polarized extension cords with polarized appliances.
- Never place an extension cord in areas where it can be tripped over.
- Make sure cords don't dangle from counters and tabletops where they can be pulled or tripped over.
- Never use an extension cord while it is coiled or looped.
- Never cover an extension cord with newspapers, clothing, or rugs, and never place an extension cord where it is likely to be damaged by foot traffic or heavy furniture.
- Don't use staples or nails to attach extension cords to baseboards or other surfaces. The cord could be damaged and present a shock or fire hazard.
- Use special, heavy-duty extension cords for high-wattage appliances such as air conditioners, electric heaters, and freezers.
- When using outdoor tools and appliances, use only extension cords designed for outdoor use. Check the label.
- Don't overload extension cords by plugging in appliances that draw a total wattage higher than the rating of the cord.
- Never plug in an extension cord where the cord is bent at a right angle to the plug by heavy furniture pushed against the wall. Instead, use special angled extension cords designed for these circumstances.
- Use only three-wire extension cords for appliances with three-prong plugs. Never remove or cut the third prong; it is a safety feature designed to reduce the risk of shock or electrocution.
- Never place extension cords under rugs.

touch a bare electrical wire by accident while another part of your body is grounded. The GFCI interrupts power faster than a wink of an eye to prevent a lethal dose of electricity from reaching you. You may receive a shock during the time it takes the GFCI to cut off the electricity, but you will not be electrocuted or receive a serious injury.

Accidents cost the United States a total of $177.2 billion in lost wages, work loss, property damage, insurance administration, and medical expenses in 1991.

Three types of GFCIs are available for home use. The first is the *receptacle type*. This device looks like a standard duplex electrical outlet except the GFCI is installed inside. It fits into the outlet box and protects you against electrocution from any appliances plugged into that particular receptacle.

The second type of GFCI is known as the *portable type*. This is used in situations where the receptacle type isn't practical although it affords the same protection. You simply plug it into the outlet then plug your appliance into it. You can also buy GFCIs already connected to an extension cord. This gives you protection when using power tools, electric lawn mowers, and other appliances outside.

The third type of GFCI is the *circuit breaker type*. In homes equipped with circuit breakers instead of fuses, this GFCI is installed in place of a circuit breaker right inside the circuit-breaker housing, protecting any wiring or appliances on the circuit to which it is connected. Often, houses have circuit-breaker GFCIs installed on circuits branches for bathroom and kitchen outlets and outlets located on patios, garages, and in crawl spaces.

If you are handy and can install an electrical outlet, you can probably install your own receptacle-type GFCI. However, don't attempt it unless you know what you're doing. Let an electrician install the circuit-breaker types. It's dangerous because you have to turn off the main electricity to the house. The portable GFCI requires no special knowledge to install.

All GFCIs have a test button you should press once a month. There will be an indicator of some sort that shows the unit is working properly. If it's not working correctly, replace it. There is also a "reset" button that will reset the GFCI to its protection status.

Hair Dryers: Selecting ■ and Using Them Safely ■

Selection
- The best protection is afforded by hair dryers that have miniature shock protectors or GFCIs. Look for this feature on the package. These hair dryers can be identified by their rectangular-shaped plugs with a "reset" button at the end of the power cord.
- If you own a hair dryer without the shock protector, make certain you always use the dryer in an outlet protected by a Ground Fault Circuit Interrupter (GFCI) or in a room where contact with water is not possible.

Using Hair Dryers Safely
- Never use a hair dryer while you are in the bathtub or standing on a wet floor.
- If you use the hair dryer near a sink, drain the sink of water **before** plugging in the dryer.
- If a hair dryer accidentally falls into water while the plug is still attached to an outlet, **be sure to unplug the cord first before** touching the dryer or water. Do not use the dryer again until it has been inspected by an appliance service center.
- Do not store a plugged-in dryer on a rack or shelf over a sink or bathtub. If it falls into the tub while someone is bathing, he or she could be electrocuted.
- Never set the hair dryer down while it is still operating. Turn it off and place it away from any water source.

Warning Signs of Electrical Problems

Electrical problems often give plenty of warning. If you pay attention to the signs, you could save your life. Some of the most important warning signs include the following:

- **Power outages.** Fuses needing replacement or circuit breakers needing resetting frequently could mean problems.

- **Dim or flickering lights or a shrinking picture on your TV** can indicate electrical problems.
- **Noises** such as sizzling sounds or buzzes from the electrical system can also indicate problems.
- **Unpleasant odors** could be from hot insulation. The smell is distinctive, best described as burning rubber or plastic.
- **An overrated panel** means your fuses or circuit breakers are rated at higher currents than the capacity of the circuits—for example, a thirty-ampere fuse in a twenty-ampere circuit. The wires could short-circuit and cause a fire before the fuse would blow. One of the most dangerous electrical activities of all is to replace a blown fuse with something other than a proper-rated fuse. Never place a penny or anything else in a fuse socket to complete the circuit. There was a reason why the fuse blew. Circumventing the fuse, especially without learning what conditions caused the fuse to blow, is extremely dangerous.
- **Damaged insulation** caused by cut, broken, burned, or cracked wires can be dangerous.
- **Electrical shock,** no matter how minor, is a warning sign of a hazardous condition.

Even if none of these warning signs is obvious, a home electrical inspection may be wise. If your last inspection was more than forty years ago, an inspection is overdue. If it was within ten to forty years ago, an inspection is advisable. If your last inspection was less than ten years ago, an inspection should not be needed unless you see any of the warning signs. How do you know when your home was last inspected? When you look at the fuse box or circuit-breaker panel box you should find an inspection date with a signature or initials on a tag or label. Sometimes it's written on the list of circuit connections found on the door of the box. Who should inspect your electrical system? Either a licensed electrician or a licensed electrical inspector.

Check Your House

Besides the early-warning signs, you should go through your house room by room and look for possible electrical problems.

Check your electrical **fixtures** first. Do not install a light bulb that exceeds the maximum wattage of the fixture (indicated on the fixture label). This is especially important for fixtures that have covers or hoods that trap heat. Sometimes you can't find a maximum-wattage label. In that case, a bulb no larger than sixty watts is often a good bet, although it's not 100 percent safe.

■ Antenna Safety ■

Follow these safety suggestions when installing or using an antenna:

- Work only in good weather. Thunderstorms, rain, moderate to heavy winds, and damp or icy ground can create hazards.
- Follow the manufacturer's instructions closely for assembling the antenna and its support mast.
- **Check carefully for overhead wires.** Don't assume that nearby wires are telephone wires. Treat all wires as if they were carrying dangerous amount of electricity, and maintain a distance of at least **twice** the length of the assembled antenna and mast from the all overhead wires.
- If you must erect or move an antenna in an area where there are overhead wires:
    - Use a nonmetal ladder (wood or fiberglass).
    - Wear rubber boots or shoes, industrial rubber gloves, and a long-sleeved shirt or jacket.
    - Ground the antenna-support structure prior to erecting. If the antenna should begin to fall (for example, if you start to lose control because of a wind gust), **go away and stay clear.** Do not touch the antenna again until you are sure it is not in contact with any overhead wires.

Check all **electrical cords** for their general condition. Look for damage, cracks in the insulation, or any other signs of deterioration. Power cords should never be knotted or tied to anything. They should never be stapled or nailed to a wall because the insulation could be cut. Never run cords under rugs or furniture legs. Pay extra attention to cords entering appliances. This is the area where they are most commonly bent and frayed.

Feel all **outlets** with your hand. **They should never be warm.** Warm outlets indicate unsafe wiring conditions. Also check that all plugs fit snugly in outlets; loose-fitting plugs can overheat. Do all your outlets have the proper covers? Exposed wiring is dangerous.

We're all guilty of doing this at one time or another but . . . **never pull cords from outlets by holding the cord and yanking.** This is the major cause of damaged cords. **Always hold the plug when removing a cord from an outlet.**

And here's another suggestion from the experts: unplug all **kitchen appliances** such as toasters, blenders, juicers, and food processors when not in use. How many of us will really do that? Only a few. It's a bother, but if you remember to do it regularly it could become a habit that saves lives. Unattended, plugged-in appliances create an unnecessary risk.

Large appliances such as washers, dryers, and dishwashers vibrate and can put stress on electrical connections. Check their cords for signs of wear. If you should ever receive an electrical shock (not just static electricity) from touching an appliance, call an electrician immediately. Don't touch it again until it's been checked.

Electric blankets should be checked for cracks or breaks in wiring especially where the wiring enters the blanket itself and also by the switch because the wires there are subject to twisting and bending. Never fold electric blankets and never cover them with anything; they could overheat.

SAFETY BY THE NUMBERS

The safest countries, based on per capita accidental death rates, are Hong Kong, Singapore, Egypt, Chile, and the Netherlands. The United States ranks twentieth.

Electricity used outdoors presents special hazards because of moisture. All outside outlets should be of the three-prong variety. Likewise, all appliances used outdoors should have three-pronged plugs. Check the outlet for moisture damage. All outside outlets should have a waterproof cover. And of course, all outside outlets should have GFCIs installed in compliance with current building codes. If your house is an older model and doesn't have GFCIs outside, consider installing them or using a portable GFCI.

Power Tools

For the most part, Harry and Harriet Homeowner hurt themselves with power tools because they're not experienced in their use. *Power tools can be dangerous!* Make sure you know what you're doing before you plug in that high-powered, fast-moving machine.

Always wear eye protection when using tools that send material or dust flying. Safety glasses are good, but safety goggles are better. People around you should also wear eye protection too.

Wear **ear protection** when necessary, especially when working for a long time in noisy areas or with noisy tools. How loud is too loud? If you have to shout to be heard by someone standing a few feet away, ear protection is indicated. Both ear muffs and ear plugs are available. A good bet is throwaway foam ear plugs that you use only once.

Dust masks or respirators are also good items to wear when there's lots of dust or mist in the work area as the result of cutting, drilling, sanding, or spray painting. Disposable, one-use masks are available as well as reusable respirators that you clean after each use.

Respirators vary based on what you're trying to keep out of your lungs. For example, a dust respirator will work well during sanding but will not do much to keep out fumes while stripping the finish from old furniture.

Hardware stores have a variety of masks for almost every application. Remember to choose the right respirator

for the job, wear the mask properly, and follow the manufacturer's instructions.

Chain Saws

More than thirty thousand people go to the hospital each
year with a chain-saw injury. Many lose a finger, a hand, or a
foot. Take the proper precautions when using a chain saw:

- Review the owner's manual frequently.
- Avoid fatigue. It can lead to accidents.
- *Always* hold a running saw with two hands.
- Start all cuts at top speed (full throttle) and continue to
  cut at top speed.
- Avoid "kickback." The saw's chain can throw the
  chain saw violently back at you when it strikes an object. This kickback occurs when the chain around the
  tip area touches any object such as a nearby log or
  branch. It can also occur when the wood being cut
  closes in and pinches the saw chain.
- Don't work alone. Use the buddy system.
- If you must cut a limb that is under tension, refer to the
  owner's manual for the proper technique. Bent limbs
  under tension can spring out as the cut is completed.
- Be sure your body is clear of the natural path that the
  saw will follow after the cut is completed.
- Turn off the saw before making any adjustments or
  repairs. *Never* rest your chain saw on your leg or knee
  or attempt to start it while it is resting on your leg or
  knee.

Lawn Mowers

We tend to overlook the dangers associated with lawn
mowers because they're an everyday tool. However, lawn
mowers are dangerous. Follow these suggestions to protect
yourself from lawn-mower injuries.

Always wear substantial shoes when operating lawn mowers; don't wear sandals or go barefooted. Heavy shoes will give provide additional protection if you should run over your foot. Be sure to clear the lawn of sticks, rocks, and other debris before mowing. Keep pets and people away when you're operating the mower.

Riding mowers require special attention. Follow these do's and don'ts to keep yourself safe while operating a riding lawn mower:

Do:
- Read the mower's instruction manual.
- Mow up and down slopes, not across.
- Slow down before turning.
- Watch for holes, ruts, and uneven terrain that can cause the mower to overturn.
- Be extra careful in tall grass. It can hide obstacles. Always check the area for toys, rocks, branches, and other debris before mowing.
- Choose a low-enough gear so that you will not have to stop or shift while on a slope.
- Keep all movement on slopes slow and gradual.
- Avoid sudden changes in speed and direction.
- Avoid starting or stopping on slopes. If tires lose traction, disengage the blades and proceed slowly straight down the hill.

Don't:
- Mow on wet grass. Reduced traction can cause sliding.
- Use a grass catcher on steep slopes.
- Try to stabilize the mower by putting your foot on the ground.
- Turn while the mower is on a slope unless it is unavoidable. If you must turn on a slope, disengage the blade, then turn slowly and gradually downhill.
- Carry passengers.
- Mow at night or at dusk unless the area is well lighted.
- Mow in reverse unless absolutely necessary.

Snow Blowers

Snow blowers are dangerous in the same way that lawn mowers are dangerous: a sharp blade is turning rapidly. When a snow blower becomes clogged with snow and ice the operator may be tempted to clear it out quickly and continue with the job. But remember: **Always turn the blower off before putting your hand anywhere near the intake area.** Placing the engine in neutral isn't safe enough. Turn off the engine before doing any clearing.

Poisons in the Home

Many poisonous products in our homes, such as pesticides, are intentionally poisonous while others are poisonous only when used improperly. Medicines are a good example of that.

SAFETY BY THE NUMBERS

On average, there are ten accidental deaths and about 960 disabling injuries every hour.

The statistics about accidental poisonings are surprising. For all accidental deaths in the home, poisoning is second only to falls, and it is the leading cause of death for those twenty-five to forty-four years old. Pesticides and medicines are responsible for many of these accidental poisonings.

Safe Pesticide Handling

Pesticides are *not* safe. They are produced specifically to be toxic to some organisms. However, by heeding all the following tips, you can reduce your risks when you use pesticides.

- All pesticides legally sold in the United States must bear a label approved by the Environmental Protection Agency. Check the label to make sure it has an EPA registration number.

- Before using the pesticide, read the label carefully. Even if you have used it before, read the label again. Don't trust your memory as to correct and proper usage.
- Use the pesticide according to the instructions. Not only is it unsafe, but it can perhaps be life threatening to use it otherwise. It is also illegal to do so.
- Before using any pesticide, know what to do in case of accidental poisoning.
- Do not use a "restricted-use" pesticide unless you are a formally trained, certified pesticide applicator. These products are too dangerous to be used without special training.
- Use only the amount directed. Twice the amount will not do twice as good a job. You could harm yourself or others by using more than the prescribed amount.
- Look for the following signal words on the label:
     Danger means highly poisonous.
     Warning means moderately hazardous.
     Caution means least hazardous.
  These signal words tell you how hazardous a pesticide is if swallowed, inhaled, or absorbed through the skin.
- Wear protective clothing if the label requires it. For example, wear long-sleeved shirts, long pants, rubber gloves, and eye protection if the label says to do so.
- If you must mix or dilute pesticides, do so outside in a well-ventilated area. Do not mix more than you need for the current application.
- Keep children and pets away from the mixing area.
- If a spill occurs, clean it up promptly. Don't wash it away (unless the labels prescribes this), but sprinkle with sawdust or kitty litter, sweep it into a plastic bag, and dispose of it according to the label.
- Remove all children's and pets' toys from the application area. Remove food, dishes, pots, and pans before treating kitchen cabinets, and wait until shelves are dry before refilling them.
- When spraying outdoors, close your windows. When spraying inside, allow adequate ventilation according

to the label directions. Leave the house for the amount of time prescribed by the label.

- Never spray or dust outdoors on a windy day.
- Never smoke while applying pesticides. Not only are some products flammable, but you could easily carry traces of the chemical from your hand to your mouth.
- Never transfer pesticides to containers not intended for them, such as empty soft-drink containers. Keep pesticides in containers that clearly mark the contents.
- Shower and shampoo thoroughly after using a pesticide. Wash your clothing separately from the regular household laundry. To prevent tracking pesticides into the house, rinse boots and shoes before entering your home.
- To remove residues from mixing tools, use a bucket to rinse the tools, then pour the rinse water into the pesticide container and reuse the solution by applying it according to the label directions.

When we think of dangers from pesticides we think of accidentally drinking the pesticide or spilling it on our skin. Another danger that can be just as unhealthy is inhaling pesticides. After applying pesticides, airborne particles can circulate throughout your house, and although all pesticides should be considered dangerous, one in particular should be paid special attention. It is *paradichlorobenzene,* which is commonly used in moth repellents. Little is known about its long-term effects on humans, but it has caused cancer in laboratory animals. The EPA requires that products containing paradichlorobenzene have a warning label that says: *avoid breathing vapors.* When using products containing this chemical, do so cautiously. When possible, place items to be protected against moth infestation in trunks or other containers that can be stored in areas that are separately ventilated from your home, such as in sheds or detached garages. Paradichlorobenzene is also used in many air fresheners and deodorizers, so be careful where you place them.

Medicines

Although manufacturers have tried to make the perfect *tamper-proof* medicine package, they really can only make a *tamper-evident* package. Therefore, vigilance is up to you. Protect yourself from over-the-counter medicines that have been tampered with by following these simple rules:

1. Read the label. Tamper-evident labels tell you what a tampered seal looks like.
2. Inspect the outer package. If there is evidence of tampering, don't buy it. Give it to store personnel so an unwary customer can't buy it.
3. After you open the package at home, examine the medicine itself. If there are any capsules that look different from the rest, don't use any of them. Notify the store. Not every change in the appearance or condition of medicine means it has been tampered with, but if you have any doubts return it to the store.
4. Never take medicine in the dark.
5. Check the medicine each time you take it. You may have missed some problems the other times you took the medicine.
6. **If you have any doubts, don't use the medicine.**

Indoor Air Pollution

Fifteen years ago there was little talk about indoor air pollution. In fact, some scientists who began researching the subject were told they were wasting their time. What could be wrong with the air inside our homes?

During the last decade this thinking has changed. Not only are many scientists researching the effects of indoor air pollution now, but the discoveries they are making are sometimes scary. Now we know there are many different sources of indoor air pollution, and some of the effects can be devastating.

For example, who would have thought that asbestos, a substance with fire-retarding properties that could save lives, could also cause lung cancer? The same could be said for formaldehyde, a chemical used in materials that help insulate our homes. Now we know formaldehyde can cause mild, nuisance irritations like coughing, skin rashes, and wheezing in some people, and it has been linked to cancer in others.

Much of the impetus for studying indoor air pollution grew out of the oil-embargo crisis in the mid-1970s. The national goal was to save energy in our homes and offices by keeping them "tight," with windows and joints that didn't leak air. Modern insulation products that used highly volatile chemical materials were employed for the first time in new homes and retrofitted to older homes.

We know that some pollution sources cause problems and symptoms immediately, while others take years to become evident. It's clear that the longer you are exposed to indoor air pollutants, the more severe your symptoms will be. We also know that those people who are chronically sick suffer more from the effects of indoor air pollution than healthy people. Last, we know that many of the causes of air pollution can be alleviated with time and effort. The keys are controlling the source of the pollution and increasing ventilation. By understanding how air enters and leaves your home, you can change your ventilation system and keep yourself safe and healthy.

Air enters and leaves your home in three ways. The first is *infiltration*, the movement of air through joints and cracks in walls and floors (basically, the holes in your house). The second method is *natural ventilation*, air traveling through open windows and doors. Third is *mechanical ventilation* in which mechanisms such as fans move air in and out of your house.

The rate at which the outdoor air replaces the indoor air is known as the *air-exchange rate*. When that rate is low, the air in your house smells stale and the amount of pollution is high. When the air-exchange rate is high, pollution levels are lower.

The average air-exchange rate for homes in the United States, according to the Environmental Protection Agency, is 0.7 to 1.0 air changes per hour. In "leaky" homes, that rate can be as high as 2.0 changes per hour and in "tight" homes it's as little as 0.2 changes per hour. A 1.0 air change per hour doesn't mean that all pollutants will be removed in one hour. The process of ventilation and pollution removal is gradual and ongoing. Also, some pollutants don't necessarily stay in the air where they can be whisked to the outdoors. Many particles drop out of the air into rugs and onto furniture where they may stay until mechanically removed by, say, a vacuum cleaner.

How can you tell if you have an indoor air pollution problem?

Sometimes it's easy. If you just moved into a new home and find that your eyes are itching and red and you're sniffling or coughing and you don't think you have a cold, your symptoms could be caused by the new surroundings. (If you move to a different part of the country, they could be caused by new pollens.) If you've just remodeled your house and added some insulation or painted and subsequently suffered some symptoms, this could be a sign of air pollution. Likewise, if you've just treated your house with pesticides and find that you're feeling fatigued, this could be a reaction to the chemicals. If you think there's a problem, consult your doctor, although many doctors don't know a lot about indoor air pollution. It's not something that's taught in medical school. Doctors do know about allergies, though, and sometimes the symptoms are similar. You might want to try an allergist. You might also contact your local health department and ask about indoor air pollution problems in your area. Often, health-department officials see the same symptoms in the same housing subdivisions because similar building materials were used in all the buildings.

Another way to judge if you have indoor air pollution problems is to seek out pollution sources such as mildew, mold, and chemicals, although having these pollutants present does not necessarily mean you're going to have a problem with them. Everyone's reaction is different, but it is a good place to start. Look for outward signs that your house has an air pollution problem. Is the air stuffy? Is the basement moist? (This could contribute to mold and mildew.) Are air filters on the furnace dirtier than you would expect them to be based on the manufacturer's instructions? For example, if the manufacturer suggests that you clean the filter every three months but it's dirty after one month, that's a strong indication of a dust problem in your house.

Before we begin to focus on individual pollutants, the obvious question is: Can you *measure* your home for pollutants? The answer is yes, but it can be expensive (except for measuring radon levels.) You will need specialists using sophisticated equipment, and even then the results could be inconclusive because there is no agreement on maximum safe levels for some pollutants. And again, everyone reacts differently to different levels. Let's look at some of the most common culprits of indoor air pollution.

Biological Pollutants

Biological pollutants are or were living organisms. These include mold (fungi), mildew, viruses, animal dander, pollen, dust mites, and bacteria.

The most common health problem related to biological pollutants is allergic reaction, including watery eyes, runny nose, sneezing, itching, coughing, headache, and fatigue, but other possible health effects include infectious diseases and toxicity. If you are prone to respiratory diseases such as asthma these pollutants can be life threatening.

The reaction that scientists know the least about is toxicity, or poisoning. There are a small number of people who are deathly hypersensitive to some biological pollutants, such as molds. For them, going into a house where these airborne pollutants exist can be fatal.

Airborne bacteria can be especially dangerous. Some bacteria, such as those that caused the condition nicknamed "Legionnaires' Disease," thrive in a building's ventilation system and can be spread to anyone inside.

Getting Rid of Biological Pollutants. Biological pollutants need two things to survive and thrive: nutrients and constant moisture with poor air circulation.

If you're susceptible to biological pollutants you should take steps to rid your house of them. *Dust control is paramount in your fight.* Keep your home clean, especially the refrigerator and food-storage areas. Insects won't come where they can't eat. Fungi need nutrition too. Firewood, for example, is a source of food for some fungi, and so are stored construction materials such as wallboard, wood, and insulation that have spent time outside where they picked up molds. Fungi can also grow on food particles.

You can't see dust mites, but they live in chairs, carpets, bedding, and other fabrics. Vacuuming can't do the entire job. If you're susceptible to dust mites, use washable rugs rather than wall-to-wall carpet. Always wash bedding in hot water (at least 130 degrees Fahrenheit) at least once a week to kill the little critters.

Vacuum and clean rooms well. Some particles are so small they can pass right through the vacuum bag and back into the room, so don't rely on vacuuming alone. Wash fabric items such as cushions and curtains whenever possible.

Physically remove mold and mildew from any surfaces. Bathrooms and kitchen counters are problem areas. Clean shower curtains with a household cleaner and rinse well before rehanging. Discard curtains if you can't get them clean. Remove all traces of mold from walls, ceilings, and floors. Don't simply paint over the surfaces; if you do, the mold will come back.

Moisture Control. Biological pollutants love moist, damp areas. Don't accommodate them. Keep them out by lowering the humidity in your house. Here are some suggestions for doing this:

- Check all pipes and faucets for leaks, and fix leaks and seepage. Keep water away from your house by redoing the landscape, making sure the ground slopes away from the foundation.
- Put a plastic cover over dirt in crawl spaces. This will keep water from evaporating and rising into your house. Make sure the crawl space is well ventilated.
- Use exhaust fans in areas where moisture is inevitable such as bathrooms, kitchens, and basements. The exhaust fan should expel air to the outside, not into the attic. In fact, your attic should have an exhaust fan as

well. Not only will it reduce pollutants but it will also keep fungi from rotting and destroying structural joists and beams. Make sure your basement has a sump pump that removes water to an outgoing sewer if water leakage is a problem you can't solve.

- Use dehumidifiers and air conditioners, especially in hot, humid climates. They take moisture out of the household air. *Caution: Clean these appliances frequently so they don't become moist sources that harbor pollutants and bacteria.*
- Open your windows and air out your house frequently.
- Pay special attention to carpeting on concrete floors, especially in basements. Carpets can absorb moisture from a cold, damp floor and breed pollutants.
- Clean the drip pan in your refrigerator often. Not only is it damp, but it contains food particles, so it is a perfect place for biological pollutants to grow.
- If rugs or carpets sustain water damage from leaks, wash them as soon as possible to prevent any mold or fungus from growing.

Radon

Radon is a colorless, odorless gas that occurs naturally and is found everywhere at very low levels. It is a by-product of the breakdown of naturally occurring uranium, and it enters homes through dirt floors, cracks in concrete floors, floor drains, and other openings.

Radon has always been with us, but concern about it first arose in the late 1960s when elevated radon levels were found in homes in the western United States that had been built with materials contaminated by waste from uranium mines. EPA studies show that as many as 10 percent of American homes may have elevated levels of radon. Areas with certain types of rock formations and certain soils go hand in hand with high radon levels.

The dangers of radon are still sketchy. The only known effect to radon exposure is lung cancer, especially in people who smoke cigarettes. EPA estimates that about five thousand to twenty thousand lung cancer deaths can be attributed to radon. It is believed that the higher the radon level and the longer you are exposed, the higher your risk.

Measuring radon levels in your home is easy and inexpensive. First, however, check with your state radiation office to ask if high levels of radon have been found in your area. Because radon is associated with certain geologic features, chances are almost zero that your house will have elevated levels if your area is not known to have high radon levels.

If your area has not been checked, or if you would like the peace of mind that a test can give, you can purchase one of two kinds of radon testers, the charcoal canister or the alpha track detector. The charcoal canister costs about ten to twenty-five dollars and takes about three to seven days for proper testing. The alpha track detector costs from twenty to fifty dollars and takes two to four weeks. Both devices work the same way. Each is exposed to the air in your home then sent to a laboratory for analysis.

You can sometimes get radon testers free from state health or radiation offices if your area is suspected of high levels. You can also buy over-the-counter devices at stores and then mail the device to a private laboratory for analysis after you take the reading. The cost for analysis is included in the cost of the device. Follow the instructions in the radon testing kit exactly.

In general, you should test for the highest radon levels by placing the testing device in the lowest living area in your home. For example, because radon gas rises, a basement would have a higher level than the third floor.

Your results will state your home's radon level in *picocuries per liter* (pCi/l) and give you guidelines about what that level indicates. In general, if your levels are above 200 pCi/l you should perform a follow-up measurement while also considering some simple actions to immediately reduce radon gas in your home (see the list below). If your measurement is 20 pCi/l to about 200 pCi/l, perform follow-up measurements for about the next three months. If your screening shows 4 pCi/l to about 20 pCi/l, make follow-up measurements for one year or weekly measurements during each of the four seasons. If your screening is less than 4 pCi/l, no follow-up is required.

Never undertake any major remedies based solely on the first measurement. Always do several follow-up measurements in different parts of the house. The true result will be their average. If follow-up measurements reveal high radon levels, consult a specialist about any course of action. In the meantime, the EPA recommends that you can lower your risk by doing the following:

- Stop smoking. Radon increases your risk of lung cancer, which is already high from smoking.
- Spend less time in high-radon areas, such as basements.
- Increase ventilation in the house, especially in the basement.
- Keep crawl spaces well ventilated.
- Repair easily fixed cracks and holes in the foundation, around drain pipes, and in basement floors.

While these are positive actions that can reduce your risks, they are not substitutes for long-term permanent fixes such as installing specially designed air exchangers and filters. These major remedies should only be performed by licensed, trained contractors. Your state radiation office should be able to give you a list of these contractors.

Asbestos

Asbestos inhalation has no immediate health effects, but as with radon, long-term exposure can lead to lung cancer, especially in smokers.

Asbestos is prevalent in insulation, pipe coverings, siding, roofing materials, fireproofing, and acoustical building materials. It was also added to some vinyl floor tiles to strengthen them. Damage to these materials exposes the raw asbestos to the air where you can breathe them into your lungs. Asbestos can be released from floor tiles if the tiles are damaged by sanding. Asbestos products are not dangerous in themselves; it's only when the asbestos fibers become airborne that a potential problem arises.

Asbestos fibers are very small, so small that they pass through the filters of vacuum cleaners and float back into the air. If you believe you see any asbestos in your home, do not disturb it. Never try to sweep or vacuum it. This will only cause the asbestos dust to spread throughout the house. Seek professional advice to determine if the substance is indeed asbestos. Use only trained and qualified contractors to handle removal of the asbestos materials. In many jurisdictions, only licensed asbestos removers can handle asbestos; no one else may do such work.

Some appliances such as toasters, dishwashers, ranges, clothes dryers, and electric blankets, contain asbestos that could be released when the appliance is used. However, the amount of asbestos released by these products is very small and generally does not constitute a health hazard. One exception was hair dryers that used asbestos heat shields and blew asbestos particles directly at the user. Currently produced hair dryers do not contain any asbestos. In 1986, the CPSC required labeling of all products containing asbestos. In 1989, the Environmental Protection Agency mandated a ban on most asbestos products, concluding in 1996, although some of these bans have been set aside by court action.

Formaldehyde

Formaldehyde gas is colorless but strong-smelling and is emitted from building materials such as plywood, particle board, and fiberboard. It's used in the adhesive that holds these materials together. This glue is called *urea-formaldehyde resin* and the resin-to-wood ratio is highest in medium-density fiberboard used in cabinets, wall paneling, and furniture tops. Formaldehyde is also found in foam insulation products, permanent-press clothing and draperies, and as a preservative in some paints.

Formaldehyde's effects can be quick and severe, ranging from throat irritation, skin rashes, and coughing, to long-term problems such as cancer, liver, and kidney damage. Some people are so sensitive to the substance they break out immediately in a rash and may incur organ damage within a few years of prolonged exposure. If you have any signs such as severe eye, nose, and throat irritation after moving to a new home leave the building until you can consult a physician or allergist.

If the levels are low enough that you aren't experiencing any severe problems but believe formaldehyde could be in the air (based on your knowledge of the building materials used) you may want to use air conditioners and dehumidifiers to maintain moderate temperatures and reduce humidity because the rate at which formaldehyde is emitted depends upon heat and humidity. Always increase ventilation after bringing new sources of formaldehyde into your home. If possible, choose "exterior grade" pressed-wood products because they generally contain phenol resins instead of urea-formaldehyde resins.

Check the label of any pressed-wood product, including cabinetry and furniture, before you purchase it. If you're sensitive to formaldehyde you should avoid bringing formaldehyde-rich products into your home.

One good thing about formaldehyde is that its emission from products diminishes sharply with time. If your home was built many years ago, it's unlikely that formaldehyde is still leaking into the air. During the 1970s many homes that were insulated with urea-formaldehyde foam insulation in the name of energy conservation soon exhibited high levels of formaldehyde, but those have since dropped to trace amounts. Unless the insulation is damp and there are cracks or openings in the walls that expose the foam, there shouldn't be a problem.

Combustion Pollutants

While gas- and wood-burning stoves and heaters pose a fire danger, as we discussed earlier, they also present a source of unhealthy, sometimes fatal, indoor air pollution. When you burn any fuel such as wood, kerosene, or oil, you produce by-products known as *combustion pollutants*. These substances include carbon monoxide, nitrogen dioxide, sulfur dioxide, and soot particles, as well as water vapor, which isn't dangerous in itself but can lead to high humidity that encourages the growth of mold and mildew.

Exposure to combustion pollutants can cause varying health problems ranging from headache and nausea to suffocation and death. The most dangerous of all combustion pollutants is carbon monoxide, an odorless, colorless gas that causes symptoms—dizziness, weakness, headaches—that may go unnoticed or mistaken for other illnesses until it's too late to recover. Carbon monoxide displaces the air in your home and also reduces your blood's ability to carry oxygen, a condition that causes suffocation. Carbon monoxide poisoning can occur rather quickly or over a long period of time, slowly deteriorating your health. If you have the symptoms of carbon monoxide poisoning listed here, see your doctor immediately. He or she can order a blood test that will determine the carbon monoxide levels in your body.

- Do symptoms only occur in your home but decrease when you're outside?
- Is anyone else at home suffering the same symptoms?
- Are your symptoms getting worse?
- Have your appliances been inspected lately?

To reduce the chances of carbon monoxide poisoning in your home, make sure all your combustion appliances are vented to the outside. **Be certain they are installed properly, inspected regularly, and used according to instructions.** These are the most important steps you can take to cut your risks of carbon monoxide poisoning because the gas is produced by improper or incomplete burning of fuel.

Lead

The health hazards of lead have been known for a long time. Lead is toxic to many of the body's organs and is linked to brain and kidney damage as well as damage to the nervous system. What makes lead especially dangerous is that small children are more vulnerable to lead exposure than adults because lead interferes with normal physical and mental development and can cause organ damage. Also, children are more apt to ingest lead indirectly because they get dust in their mouths during play. Fetuses are also at risk in a lead-rich environment.

Until the ban on leaded gasoline, automobile gas was the prime source of airborne lead. With that source curtailed, (although some ground near highways still contains high levels of lead from exhaust) attention is still focused on lead-based paint, which is found in many older homes. This old paint can easily chip and be eaten by children, and its dust can be inhaled.

About two-thirds of the houses built before 1940 and about one-third of homes built from 1940 through 1960 contain leaded paint. Leaded paint has been used in some homes since 1960 but not a large number. If you think your home has leaded paint, you should have it tested. Consult your state or municipal health department for advice on certified testers in your area.

If you have lead paint in your home and it is in good condition and there is little chance of it being eaten by children you may want to leave it alone. As long as dust from the paint doesn't get into the air, you are in no danger. (In some areas, selling a home with lead paint is against the law. You must have the paint removed before sale.) Do not paint over lead paint because preparing the surface by sanding or removing cracked paint can produce lead dust. Some small painted areas can be safely covered by wallpaper, but seek advice from a lead expert before beginning such work.

If conditions are such that lead removal is necessary, check your local ordinances. Many areas require that lead-removal workers be specially trained and certified by the government. While your house is being "deleaded," no one other than the workers should be in the house.

If you've recently been exposed to lead dust, you should be tested. A simple blood test will tell you about possible elevated levels. However, if exposure has been in the past, a blood test may not be definitive. Your physician may suggest neurological testing.

Another source of lead is from plumbing. Lead finds its way into drinking water from lead used to solder pipe joints. If your house is old, it may have these lead joints. You should have your water checked for lead if you believe there may be a problem with your pipes.

For most homes, running the tap for a few minutes will flush out any high levels of lead that may have collected overnight in stagnated water or during longer periods of non-use.

CHAPTER

Risky Business: Hazards in the Workplace

IN 1991, ALMOST 10,000 people died on the job, and 1.7 million people suffered disabling injuries while earning a living. You don't have to work in one of the so-called dangerous industries such as mining or construction to be injured at work. Even modern, well-maintained, and well-appointed offices may have unhealthy aspects.

Just as homes may have indoor air pollution dangers, so may offices. In fact, offices sometimes have more problems because the windows in most modern building do not open for ventilation. As you may remember from Chapter 1, ventilation plays a large role in reducing indoor air pollution.

Some well-identified diseases common to office buildings—including Legionnaires' Disease, asthma, and humidifier fever—can, for the most part, be alleviated by changing some particular building condition. For example, standing water in building ventilation systems that contributes to Legionnaires' Disease can be prevented by changing the ventilation system's design and making sure water does not stagnate anywhere.

Generally speaking, office air pollution is the result of three conditions. The first is pollution sources similar to those we find in homes, for example, formaldehyde from rugs, drapes, and furniture; biological sources in rugs; and asbestos. However, office buildings also have their own unique pollutant sources not usually found at home. Copy machines, print shops, restroom cleansers and deodorizers, as well as industrial-strength cleaners are commonly found in offices.

The second source is related to ventilation systems, which are often designed to save energy by recirculating indoor air instead of bringing in large amounts of fresh, outside air. This recirculated air carries health hazards. In addition to this inherent problem, vents delivering fresh air are sometimes blocked by stacks of paper, filing cabinets, and other equipment or supplies that keep the fresh air from reaching the building's occupants. In downtown offices, air-intake vents sometimes suck large amounts of car and truck exhaust into the buildings.

The third source of pollution is caused by misuse of the building. For example, an office building's ventilation system may not be designed to handle exhaust from print shops, coffee shops, or underground parking areas because these services were not the original intent of the builder. These sources of indoor air pollution are common in buildings that have been completely renovated—except for the ventilation system.

SAFETY BY THE NUMBERS

Work accidents cost the United States $63.3 billion in 1991.

Frequently, office workers complain of common ailments that are not easily traced to one particular source. These diseases only occur in or are precipitated by being in the building, and in most cases symptoms subside or disappear when the workers leave the building. Often, large numbers of workers come down with the same symptoms. This group of diseases is known as *sick-building syndrome,* a rather vague moniker for a pollution source not easily identified. The symptoms often are sneezing, dry or burning mucous membranes in the nose, throat, and eyes, lethargy, headache dizziness, nausea, and irritability.

Finding the source of occupants' discomfort is difficult and requires investigators to interview people who are sick as well as those who are not affected. It is also necessary to inspect the design and condition of the ventilation system in an attempt to discover the causes.

If you are suffering any sick-building diseases, contact

■ Laser Printers ■

Some laser printers and copiers can produce toxic ozone gas. The source is the high-voltage system that transfers toner to the printing drum. Small amounts of ozone are produced every time an image is made. Not all laser printers or copiers produce the gas. Those using a roller-transfer system—which does not create a high-voltage field—do not produce ozone.

To combat this problem, some laser devices have ozone filters, which should be replaced periodically because they accumulate dust and dirt. There is no rule of thumb on how often to replace these filters, so check with the manufacturer. (Some laser printers have the ozone filter built into the toner. When you change the toner cartridge, you're also replacing the ozone filter.)

Asthmatics and those with pulmonary trouble may be particularly sensitive to ozone even at low levels, and some healthy people may exhibit symptoms such as headaches, nausea, and dizziness, but it's rare at the low levels produced by laser devices.

Proper ventilation of an office space will take care of most of the workers, but the other precautions mentioned in this chapter also should be taken. Never place a laser device in a closed, unventilated closet, and never sit with the exhaust blowing in your face.

---

your physician. You should also talk with the company's physician or safety officer so your input can be added to any other workers' complaints. Discuss your symptoms with co-workers, your supervisor, union representative, and others, and make sure a record is being kept of complaints. Only by collecting many complaints can authorities hope to identify the source of the illnesses. For example, if only people on the fifth floor are becoming ill, it's a pretty good bet that the source of pollution is on that floor and not building-wide. This might rule out a problem with the ventilation system (unless the fifth floor gets its own air).

Get the building managers involved. Perhaps they will hire an investigator who is knowledgeable about such problems to help find the source of pollution. Keep in mind that these detectives may not be able to pinpoint the problem as quickly as you might like. Modern buildings have so many variables and the field is so new that much of the work is done by trial and error. Because the pollution levels are usually low, measuring equipment may not help much. Recently, some government workers at the Washington, D.C. offices of the Environmental Protection Agency came down with sick-building syndrome. It took weeks for health investigators to pinpoint the cause of workers' illnesses, which ranged from sneezing and fatigue to nausea and lung discomfort. The problem turned out to be chemicals used in the processing of carpeting that had just been installed. EPA had no choice but to rip up and discard hundreds of yards of new carpet.

SAFETY BY THE NUMBERS

The third leading cause of non-accident-related work deaths is homicide.

The National Institute for Occupational Safety and Health (NIOSH) also may be able to help you. Contact NIOSH by calling 800–35NIOSH for information about obtaining a health hazard evaluation of your office. Your local or state health department may also have people on staff who can assist you in determining the cause of your sick building.

■ **OSHA** ■

The Occupational Safety and Health Act of 1970 is probably the most important law affecting worker safety in the United States. The act requires employee safety standards designed to prevent accidents, injuries, and death in the workplace. The law also requires businesses to monitor worker accidents and illnesses and establish worker-education programs. In addition, the act established two agencies: The Occupational Safety and Health Administration (OSHA), the group within the U. S. Department of Labor responsible for administration, inspections, and enforcement, and NIOSH, part of the Department of Health and Human Services that conducts research and education on worker safety. The act also called on individual states to adopt OSHA laws of their own to complement the federal laws.

In theory, businesses are supposed to comply with all regulations regarding worker safety or face penalties and fines from OSHA. But OSHA's enforcement record has been inconsistent. Sometimes enforcement is lax, while other times it's been unreasonably stringent. The result has been that since the early 1970s, workers' safety has not always been protected.

Through the years, OSHA has established safety regulations for specific industries unique to those industries' situations. Mining and petrochemicals are good examples, but the main point of OSHA's regulations is that all workers have the right to work in a safe environment.

It behooves all employers to follow the letter and spirit of the OSHA regulations. It also should be the responsibility of all employees to understand their rights under OSHA and make sure working conditions are as safe as possible.

All workers should familiarize themselves with the OSHA rules that govern their industry. These laws are available from companies and also available from OSHA offices. If you believe your company is not in compliance, work through your chain of command, your union, or whatever mechanism is available at your workplace to help set things right. You also have the right to file a complaint directly with OSHA (which may or may not lead to an inspection of your workplace, depending on how OSHA decides to handle the case).

Because technology moves faster than government, worker-safety regulations may not give workers full protection. For example, although new chemicals may seem safe, long-term effects may not yet be known. Or, as is the case with computers and video display terminals (VDTs), the use of work devices has exploded so quickly that legislators are still waiting for reliable data before deciding on what action to take. In addition, although a company may endeavor to keep its facility safe, problems may exist that the company is unaware of until it is notified by an employee. So it is up to workers to be vigilant and take responsibility for their job safety as well as enjoy the benefits of their employers' efforts.

SAFETY BY THE NUMBERS

Thirty-five million work days were lost in 1991 because of work-related accidents.

Computers

No occupational condition has caused as much controversy in recent years as the use of computers and VDTs. Use of computer keyboards has been linked to muscular problems in necks, arms, legs, fingers, and backs as well as other areas. The VDTs themselves have been blamed for eyestrain, blurred vision, cataracts, headaches, neurological diseases, and even miscarriages and cancer.

Researchers still don't know all the answers to our health questions about computers and VDTs, but studies are being conducted globally in an attempt to understand why these devices are causing their users discomfort. The main impediment to the research is that personal computers haven't been around long enough to glean definitive, long-term data. In 1976, for example, only about 675,000 VDTs were in use in the United States. By 1986, more than twenty-eight million were being used. In addition, workers using computers have widely different working conditions, and some workers exhibit symptoms quickly while others work years before problems surface. Still others show no symptoms at all.

Muddying the waters even further is the fact that workers are generally using personal computers more than in the past, sometimes sitting in front of the machines for an entire eight- or ten-hour work shift without moving away except for short intervals. This is a new variable that makes consistent, long-term data difficult to obtain. Are the problems associated with the machines themselves or the amount of time spent using them? Time spent in front of the machines appears to be a crucial factor, but research is still inconclusive.

Some recent studies *are* giving us clues about computer and VDT-related illnesses and what we can do to alleviate some of the problems. Remember, the jury is still out on specifics, so the following discussions are simply guidelines based on the best available information.

Eyestrain

Eyestrain is one of the most frequently reported symptoms by those who use computers. The American Optometric Association reports that 40 percent of complaints from VDT-using workers are from workplace factors. Visual problems can be caused by glare off the screen, one of the most common conditions. If you see glare on your screen, change the position of your work station so windows are at right angles to the screen, close the blinds, or try an anti-glare screen on the VDT that acts as a filter (much like polarizing sunglasses) to cut reflection.

Many people find they can alleviate eyestrain by changing the color scheme of the screen itself to make it more like the copy material they're reading from. For example, if you are working with "hard copy" that is composed of black print on white paper, altering your word-processing program to produce black letters on a white screen may help. Some word-processing software products, such as WordPerfect, allow you to change the screen display to almost any color combination you want. The screen and document holder should be about the same distance from your eyes. This will also prevent constant changes in eye focusing, which can cause eyestrain. And don't overlook the obvious factors of adjusting screen brightness and contrast to reduce eyestrain and fatigue. One of the keys to comfort is adjusting all factors to suit your size and working habits. It makes sense, then, that all screens, document holders, and keyboards should be on adjustable stands that allow you to customize their position.

Perhaps the single most important item you can do to alleviate computer-related eye problems is take a break. NIOSH recommends a fifteen-minute rest after two hours of continuous VDT work under moderate visual demands, and a fifteen-minute break after one hour of continuous VDT work where there is high visual demand or repetitive work tasks. This doesn't necessarily mean a rest break; you can do other work such as filing and copying.

One issue that has not yet been resolved is that of radiation emissions from VDTs. Do the low-level, low-frequency electromagnetic radiations from VDTs cause a health risk? Like much in the field of occupational health and computers, there are no definitive answers. Clearly, the emissions are of extremely low levels, but the long-term effects of these emissions, if any, are not known. (The same question can be asked about sitting in front of a TV for long periods of time.) To be on the safe side, some workers have increased their distance from VDTs, and some pregnant workers have asked to be assigned to non-VDT work during their pregnancy. New studies are being published all the time in the United States and elsewhere, and employees and employers alike should keep abreast of the latest information.

Repetitive Stress Injuries

Repetitive stress injuries (RSIs) strike an estimated 185,000 factory and office workers a year in the United States, according to the Department of Labor. These injuries account for more than half the country's occupational illnesses, compared with about 20 percent only ten years ago. (Part of this increase is because of better reporting.) An RSI is caused by using the same muscles and tendons for the same task for long periods of time.

A typical sufferer might be an auto-factory worker who screws in the same three screws on cars on the assembly line for an entire shift. Meat packers are also victims because they use the same cutting motions thousands of times a day. Both of these jobs also require a considerable amount of strength to be applied during the activity, exacerbating the condition. Other workers at high risk are garment workers, carpenters, machine operators, letter sorters, and electronic assemblers. However, the fastest growing group of RSI sufferers is white-collar workers who labor over computer keyboards.

One common RSI is carpal tunnel syndrome, which affects the area through which the median nerve travels through the wrist into the hand. This nerve provides the sense of touch in the thumb, index finger, middle finger, and half of the ring finger. When irritated, tendons housed in the carpal tunnel swell and press against the nearby median nerve, which causes tingling, numbness, and severe pain. Sometimes the sufferer can't hold things or even make a fist. If the condition isn't alleviated, it can lead to permanent nerve damage, loss of touch, and even partial paralysis.

If you have symptoms of carpal tunnel syndrome or any other RSI, stop work immediately and seek medical attention from a physician who is knowledgeable about occupational health and RSI in particular. Continued work can lead to permanent and irreversible damage.

The leading cause of accident-related work deaths is from motor-vehicle accidents. Falls and poisons follow.

The field of ergonomics studies how workers and their tasks can be made more compatible. The goal of ergonomics is to adapt the workplace and work to the worker by changing workplace design, safety features, lighting, furniture design, and sometimes employees' tasks to account for workers' limitations and capabilities. By implementing ergonomic techniques, companies can greatly increase workers' health and safety. In fact, some of the causes of RSI can be virtually eliminated by the latest ergonomic methods.

For computer workers, ergonomic design of the workspace is critical. As we've already stated, all parts of the computer workstation should be adjustable. That includes chairs, tables, computers, VDTs, and anything else in the area. Let's take these variables separately because each is important in the overall picture.

Chair. This may be the most important factor in preventing illness and disease. Simply put, your chair must fit you. Adjust the chair height so the entire sole of your foot can rest on the floor (or a footrest if you're short). The back of your knee should be slightly higher than the seat of the chair. This allows blood to freely circulate. If your feet or legs are "falling asleep," adjust the chair height might take care of it. The seat itself, the part where you place your backside, should be slightly concave with a rounded, "waterfall" edge. This design will keep you from slipping forward and also help to distribute your weight. The backrest is another crucial area. It should support the entire back, not just the middle of your back. It should be comfortable and allow you to move around a little. Your chair should have armrests to help you get up without straining your back and also provide support for your arms while typing.

Table. The table height should allow room for legs and feet to move without cramping. The best tables have a detachable holder that allows you to adjust the position of the keyboard.

Keyboard. The position of keyboard, as we've said, should be adjustable for your comfort. Most people prefer it to be flat and at or just below elbow level. If the keyboard is too close or too far from you, it can lead to cramping and fatigue. Your elbows should be relaxed, at about a right angle, and your wrists should be relaxed in a neutral position. Fingers should be slightly curled.

Mouse. Intense and prolonged usage of the computer pointer, or mouse, can cause RSI problems such as carpal tunnel syndrome. Mice come in different sizes and shapes. Choose one that fits your hand. It should be placed on a pad on the same surface as the keyboard with room to maneuver it comfortably. Make sure the surface is wide enough to allow a comfortable hand, wrist, and arm motion.

VDT. The screen should be at about eye level or slightly lower. Your head should be squarely over your shoulders without straining toward or away from the screen. Your neck and shoulders should be relaxed as you work.

Use these suggestions as starting points. It will take a while before you learn to position your work-station components to cause minimal stress on your body. Above all, take frequent breaks from one specific repetitive task. This will not only allow you to do your best work, it will also prevent injuries.

Preventing RSIs in Non-Computer Users

Because of the increased awareness of computer-industry RSIs, many employers in other industries are beginning to understand the importance of preventing these injuries, and they're learning that it's good business to give workers more breaks. RSIs can be reduced or eliminated by resting muscles and by changing tasks so that one set of muscles is not overworked. Muscles thrive and strengthen with exercise, but they can be traumatized by very repetitive, high-stress work. By rotating tasks that use different muscle groups you may eliminate RSI.

The highest rate of deaths from work accidents is in the agricultural sector. Mining/quarrying and construction follow.

But what about workers who can't change tasks, such as carpenters who have no choice but to hammer nails all day? There are several solutions. First, use powered hand tools whenever possible to alleviate muscle strain and reduce repetitive motions. Second, use tools that are designed to alleviate twisting muscles in a damaging manner. For example, tools should be lightweight and handles should allow a relaxed grip so wrists can remain straight. Handles should be shaped so they contact the largest possible surface of the inner hand and fingers. Avoid tools with sharp edges and corners. To reduce vibrations, special absorbent rubber sleeves can be fitted over tool grips.

Some workers are slow to accept new tool designs and work habits because they perceive them as "wimpy" or nontraditional. They should understand that what was acceptable in the past is no longer relevant. Today's workers put in more hours on more repetitive projects than any workers in history. Their productivity is higher than any in the past, too, but without modern technology they will suffer modern diseases.

Other Dangerous Workplace Conditions

Because each occupation has its own inherent dangers, it's impossible in one book to discuss all of them. *Your best sources of safety information are the specific industry guidelines provided by the federal and state OSHA offices.* However, some common work-related conditions can occur in widely varied occupations. In this section, we'll look at some of the most common work-related health problems.

Stress

Stress is a major factor in many job-related accidents. If you suffer from stress you may be fatigued, lose concentration, and even suffer blackouts and be unable to handle some of the risky aspects of your job. This is especially true for professional drivers, construction and petrochemical workers, machine operators, and others in high-stress industries who must constantly be "heads-up" sharp to perform their tasks safely.

SAFETY BY THE NUMBERS

The leading cause of work injury in 1988 was from overexertion; being struck by an object or striking an object was second. Falls were third.

All of us have stress in our lives at one time or another, and each of us handles it differently. Some people seem to thrive on stress and rise to the occasion (I say *seem to,* because it catches up with them eventually) while others fall apart immediately at the smallest consequences of daily life. What's important is that we recognize stress and deal with it when it becomes disruptive— before it becomes chronic.

Stress manifests itself in different ways. The most common outward symptoms of chronic stress are migraine headaches, insomnia, fatigue, irritability, and backaches. Inside your body, stress can lead to high blood pressure and possibly heart attack. There is also growing anecdotal evidence that stress is linked to ulcers, strokes, change in blood composition, and deterioration of internal organs.

While none of us can ever hope to be completely free of stress, we can reduce stress so it isn't a significant factor in our lives. Here are some tips for cutting the stress in your life:

- **Try physical activity.** Your mind gives signals to your body. When you're under stress, exercise or physical activity will relieve muscle tenseness, which in turn will tell your mind to relax.
- **Know your limits.** Learn to accept problems or situations that are beyond your control. This is easier said than done, and you may need help on this from others, which leads us to suggest that you . . .
- **Share your stress.** Seek help from a spiritual leader

or someone you trust. Just starting to share can relieve some stress.

- **Do something different.** Taking a vacation or just a "mental-health day off" can do wonders to break the cycle of stress. Getting away also gives you the opportunity to reflect on your job and your "real life," which you wouldn't notice while you're caught up in day-to-day living. After a vacation, even a one-day break, you may find that problems aren't as big as they seemed before.
- **Handle large tasks one by one or in small bites.** Trying to do too much all at once is stressful. If you have large jobs, tackle them a little at a time and above all don't take on more than you can really handle. Learn to prioritize. Do important tasks first and let other jobs wait. (This is tough for many of us.)
- **Keep yourself fit and healthy.** Get plenty of rest and eat nutritiously. Stress is amplified when you're unhealthy.
- **Find a release.** How about a good cry? How about a new hobby? Read a book. Putter around in the backyard. Anything that you find restful or fun can help reduce your stress level.
- **Learn to relax.** This is a hard one. Most of us don't know how to relax because no one ever told us how. There are many books, videos, and audio tapes on relaxation techniques. Try them; they work. Deep breathing is an important aspect of relaxation, and so is imagining yourself in a serene setting. Your goal is to learn how to "just be" without having to produce anything but your own stillness.

Back Injuries

More American workers hurt their backs on the job than any other work-related injury. More than $15 billion annually are lost in production and disability payments due to back injuries. This is the single highest workers' compensation expense according to the Department of Labor.

SAFETY BY THE NUMBERS

The most injured body part in work-related accidents is the back.

Back injuries cut across all job lines. Whether you work in a mine, a factory, or an office, knowing how to lift heavy items correctly can save your back and prevent a lifetime of pain and suffering.

You should ask your employer if he or she can make a back-injury-prevention program available to you and your co-workers. Many groups, including the American Red Cross, offer these on-the-job courses.

To safely lift an item:

1. Size up the load. Can you lift it? If not, get someone else to help you or use a machine to lift it.
2. Stand close to the load with your feet about eight to twelve inches apart for good balance.
3. Bend your knees and lift using your leg and back muscles but mainly your legs. Remember: your legs are stronger than your back.
4. Lift straight up, evenly and slowly. Push with your legs. Keep the load close to your body.
5. Get into carrying position. Don't twist your body until you're standing erect.
6. Make sure your path is clear, then turn your feet before turning your body to go in the desired direction.
7. Set the load down slowly and evenly by bending your knees and using your leg and back muscles (but mainly the leg muscles.) Don't drop the load. Let go of it gently once it's on the floor.

CHAPTER

A Report Card on School Safety

YOU DON'T HAVE to be a scholar to know that schools aren't what they used to be. Today's schoolchildren must cope with problems unheard-of just a generation ago: asbestos, deteriorating and unsafe playground equipment, and violence, to name a few. In this chapter we'll look at some ways you can ensure your child's safety while he or she is at school.

Asbestos

Because of the age of many of America's school buildings, concern over asbestos takes on a critical dimension. Thanks to federal and state legislation, however, concern over asbestos has been recognized and addressed in most of our children's schools.

In 1986, the Congress passed the Asbestos Hazard Emergency Response Act (AHERA) to protect children and school employees from asbestos exposure. We won't go into the causes and effects of asbestos—we already discussed them in Chapter 1—but we will talk about what parents can do to make sure their children are not at risk.

AHERA requires that all public and private schools be inspected for both *friable* and *nonfriable* asbestos. Friable asbestos is the kind that easily crumbles to dust, perhaps when somebody touches it. This is the most dangerous form because the asbestos fibers are carried in the air. Nonfriable asbestos is found in items such as vinyl-asbestos floor tile; these fibers won't reach the air unless someone purposely sands or cuts the tile. AHERA calls for schools to develop and implement plans to manage asbestos in a timely fashion. It also requires that schools notify parents about asbestos measures being undertaken and allow parents and teachers to become involved in the programs.

As a parent, you should make sure your children's school does the following:

- Designates and trains a person to oversee asbestos-related activities.
- Reinspects all school areas for asbestos on an ongoing basis.
- Prepares and implements an asbestos-management program.
- Uses accredited, licensed, professional asbestos evaluators and removers.
- Keeps parents and the public informed about asbestos programs.
- Makes sure all school-maintenance people know about asbestos areas that should not be disturbed when cleaning, changing light bulbs, etc.

According to AHERA, asbestos-removal programs were to be published by all schools no later than July 1989, and implementation was to be undertaken at the earliest possible time. Currently, most schools in America are free of friable asbestos (some have been closed for repairs) although some may still contain nonfriable asbestos. Although nonfriable asbestos does not present an immediate danger, all parents should be aware of the condition of their school buildings so that any asbestos, friable or not, that is apt to become damaged in areas frequented by children can be dealt with quickly and effectively. The key to children's safety is for parents to remain informed.

Playgrounds

According to the Consumer Product Safety Commission (CPSC), the overwhelming majority of playground injuries involve falling from equipment to the ground rather than from one part of the equipment to another. Other hazards involve being hit by swings and other moving apparatus, colliding with stationary equipment, and coming in contact with sharp edges, hot surfaces, and pinch points.

Accepting these facts, it becomes apparent that the most important safety factors for playgrounds are a soft surface and well-designed equipment.

The surface is of greatest importance, not only for public playgrounds but for your own play equipment at home. One of the best materials is bark mulch. A depth of twelve inches would be ideal, but six or seven inches of mulch will work well unless it gets extra-heavy use. The higher the equipment and the more people who use it, the deeper the mulch layer must be. The mulch should not be laid on a hard surface, such as cement. Mulch requires maintenance and replacement because it gets compressed during children's play. Sand is also a possible cushioning material, but it tends to compress sooner than mulch, especially after it gets wet.

Not recommended are asphalt, concrete, soil, and grass. These surfaces don't have enough shock-absorbing characteristics to be safe.

SAFETY BY THE NUMBERS

More than 200,000 injuries were sustained on playground equipment in 1989 according to the Consumer Product Safety Commission.

There are no federal regulations about playground equipment and design, but some states and municipalities have their own rules and guidelines for playgrounds. However, the CPSC has published guidelines for playground equipment with specific recommendations for the sizes and designs that enhance safety. These criteria are very complex and technical and are aimed at playground designers. If your community or school is buying a playground set, you should inquire if the design adheres to CPSC recommendations. If not, find out what design criteria are being met.

If you're buying a set for family use, check out the equipment firsthand. Don't buy a play set without seeing it. Note the design and tubing. Does it look strong? Are the bolts and nuts made of strong material? Are there any pinch points where children's necks, fingers, or other body parts can get caught? Are there any sharp points or sharp edges? Is there adequate clearance for swings and other swinging equipment? Are the pieces adjustable or interchangeable so the play set can still accommodate your child as he or she grows?

Playground equipment should be checked weekly for loose parts and wear. Check the posts for sturdiness. Wooden posts also should be checked for rot where they contact the ground. Be aware that most wood used in playground equipment is pressure treated and contains chemicals such as arsenic salts, which are toxic if swallowed. Also be aware that splinters of wood containing these chemicals may cause wounds greater than wounds caused by splinters from chemical-free wood. Check with your doctor if your children cut themselves on wooden playground equipment.

Teach your children how to use the equipment safely. In addition, be sure your children understand which components are suitable for them; what's okay for older children may not be suitable for younger children. If you have children of different ages playing in the same area, make sure each one knows which equipment he or she can use and which components are off-limits until the child gets older. The equipment should change to suit children as they get older. Older children playing on equipment designed for younger children may break the equipment or wear it out until it becomes dangerous for the tots to use.

In addition to these suggestions, go over the following safety guidelines with your child before he or she uses specific playground equipment:

Swings
- Sit in the center of the swing. Never stand or kneel.
- Hold on with both hands, and don't get off until the swing stops.

- Never twist the swing or move it from side to side.
- Never walk in front of a moving swing.

Slides
- Use the steps. Don't climb up the slide.
- Check the slide's temperature before you slide. Metal slides get very hot in direct sunlight.
- Never slide down if someone is at the bottom.
- Always slide down feet first.

Climbing Apparatus (monkey bars)
- Use both hands.
- Wear rubber-soled shoes.
- Don't climb if it's wet. You may slip.
- Watch out for people above you. Be careful of swinging feet or feet coming down on your hands.

All children and adults should be aware of the dangers of clothing with ropes and hoods that can catch on the playground equipment. Children have strangled themselves in this way, and some schools will not permit such clothing on the playground.

Amusement Rides

While we're on the subject of playgrounds and play equipment, let's discuss amusement rides. Before going on any ride, make sure it complies with safety regulations set forth by your jurisdiction. A safety-inspection certificate should be posted.

As a parent, make sure you read the posted rules. Observe age, height, and weight restrictions. Explain the safety rules to your children. Tell them to keep their hands and legs inside the ride and to keep all safety equipment such as belts and harnesses engaged until the ride is completely over.

Before your child rides, check out the operator. Does he or she seem alert and aware of the ride operation? Watch the patrons' reaction too. Are they enjoying themselves, or are they uncomfortable due to operator error? For example, are people being jolted when the ride is supposed to be gentle?

Ask the operator to stop the ride if your child shows signs of distress.

Violence

Violence has become an everyday occurrence in many schools whether they are in the cities, suburbia, or rural areas. Sheltering your children from crime may seem like the right approach, but it ignores the realities of our everyday world. Instead, parents are wise to teach their children how to cope with violence when it occurs.

Consult Chapter 5 for crime-prevention tips that apply to everyone. In this section we will specifically address school crime and violence that require additional measures such as these:

SAFETY BY THE NUMBERS

More than seventy-five students and teachers have been shot and killed in school and more than two hundred have been wounded since 1986 according to the Department of Justice.

- Encourage your children to talk to you about troubling incidents at school whether or not they're involved. This should be your first indication of problems.
- Get involved in the security measures at your child's school. Know what the school is doing to safeguard students' safety. Question anything that doesn't seem smart or well-thought-out. You may not be a security expert, but you can bring a parent's view and a common-sense approach to problems.
- Teach your children to keep away from strange children as well as adults and to back away from confrontation. If your child encounters a threatening problem in school, he or she should tell a teacher immediately.
- There's a fine line between being paranoid and being

alert. Teach your children to recognize potentially dangerous situations and to run away or scream— whatever it takes to protect themselves and get out of that situation.

- Encourage your children to walk in groups to and from school and also while inside the building.
- Teach your children their phone number and how to use the phone to call you or the police. They should know they can call anytime there's a problem.
- If your children are victims of violence, make sure they know they are not only victims but survivors. They have done nothing to be ashamed of; it wasn't their fault. Report all incidents to school authorities and the police immediately.

SAFETY BY THE NUMBERS

According to the Department of Justice, about one in five students claims to bring a dangerous weapon to school every day.

School Buses

In 1992, New Jersey became the first state to require students to wear seat belts on school buses to help prevent injuries in case of collision. Other states are following suit.

Although wearing seat belts is a good first step and makes perfect sense, it's important to realize that about two-thirds of the fatalities in school-bus accidents occur *outside* the bus when students are boarding or leaving. Despite the fact that all states require motorists to stop whenever a school bus stops, too often students are still hit by cars or even by the bus they've just left.

The most effective way to curtail these accidents is to have an adult escort students on and off the bus. In some areas, the bus driver is assigned this job. Some jurisdictions may require that the bus driver count students as they leave the bus and count them again once they've reached the sidewalk. This laborious procedure is not practical in many areas, but it does work.

About seventy-seven hundred pupils were injured in school-bus accidents in 1991.

The key to bus safety is for parents to become involved in the procedures used by their school district's bus system and make sure it is using the most effective safety measures possible. In addition, parents and children should learn the following elements of bus safety:

Boarding
- Line up in single file.
- Stay off the street until the bus has stopped.
- No pushing or shoving. No playing around.

Riding
- Follow the driver's instructions.
- Hold books, lunch boxes, and other items on your lap; don't put them in the aisle. Someone might trip.
- Don't distract the driver by causing a disturbance, making noise, or fighting.
- Stay in your seat.
- Never stick anything out of the windows, including your arms.
- Stay seated until the bus stops.

Departing
- Leave in single file, holding on to the handrail. No playing around.
- If you have to cross the street, walk along the sidewalk until the driver motions to you that it's safe to cross. Look both ways to make sure there no cars or trucks are coming toward you.
- If you drop something anywhere around the bus, don't run back to pick it up. If you left something on the bus, don't run back to get it. Stay on the sidewalk until the driver sees you. Motion and yell to the driver that you left something, and wait until he or she tells you to come over to the bus.

- Beware of the bus backing up. If you need to walk behind the bus, wait until it leaves. Never walk behind a bus unless it's parked and the engine is off.
- Get off at the bus stop closest to your house. This will minimize the number of streets you must cross.

School Laboratories

School laboratories are usually safe places. Generally speaking, instructors are cautious about stocking and using chemicals that can be dangerous. In addition, the trend in schools is to use as little of a chemical as necessary for the experiment to work.

At the beginning of each semester, students should receive laboratory safety instructions. Go over these instructions with your child, and encourage him or her to ask the teacher about anything that is unclear. Make sure your child understands that there's nothing to be ashamed of by asking. In addition, go over these general principles with your children about their behavior in the laboratory:

- Always wear lab coats or aprons to protect your clothing and yourself.
- Wear eye protection at all times.
- Don't use any equipment you haven't been told how to use. If you're unsure, ask the teacher.
- Never put your fingers to your mouth or face.
- Never eat food in labs unless the teacher okays it.
- Never sit on a lab table unless you're sure it's clean and free of chemicals and the instructor okays it.
- Never mix any chemicals unless instructed to do so.
- Make sure the ventilation hood works each time it's turned on.
- Know what to do if a fire breaks out.
- Know what to do if you get chemicals in your eyes.
- Learn the correct way to smell chemicals. Don't put your face near any test-tube or beaker.
- Never use any glassware that is cracked.

- Always wash your hands at the end of class.
- Don't take any chemicals or equipment home unless the instructor okays it.
- Never wear contact lenses in the lab because vapors, gases, and fluids can get trapped between your eyes and the lenses. Some gas-permeable lenses are considered safer than other types, but it's best not to risk it. Check with your teacher about wearing lenses in class.

CHAPTER

Safety in Motion

WRITING A CHAPTER on safety in motion is like trying to condense the wisdom of the ages on the head of a pin. All I can do is focus on only the most crucial information. As a result, this chapter is not a driver's education course. Nor is it a course on every type of accident that can happen when you travel. What I hope to do instead is show you the most common types of accidents so you can be wary of them because many are preventable.

For example, I'll share with you the three simple things that could reduce your chances of having a fatal car accident by about 80 percent! Even when accidents are due to the actions of other people and thus are not preventable, you can lessen their impact by knowing what to do once the accident occurs.

In addition to the most common types of moving accidents I've also outlined several accidents that may not happen very often but are so easy to prevent or mitigate that not knowing this information would be a shame.

So, strap yourself in .

The Three Most Important Things You Can Do to Save Your Life

When you're looking at motor-vehicle accidents, several factors scream out loud and clear:

- About half of all traffic fatalities involve alcohol.
- Passenger restraints (lap and shoulder belts) are 45 percent effective in preventing fatalities, 50 percent effective in preventing moderate to critical injuries, and 10 percent effective in preventing minor injuries.
- When speed increases, so do injuries and fatalities. Individual state studies have shown that with increasing speed limits from fifty-five miles per hour to sixty-five miles per hour come increases in fatalities by about 20 percent, serious injuries by about 40 percent, and moderate injuries by about 25 percent.

The message is simple: Don't drink, wear your seat belt, and don't exceed the speed limit. If you do these three things, you will significantly increase your chances of being accident-free. And if you are in an accident while following these suggestions, you will greatly enhance your chances of escaping serious injury or death.

SAFETY BY THE NUMBERS

Motor-vehicle-related incidents are the number one cause of accidental death and injuries in the United States.

Handling Nasty Drivers

Defensive driving is a phrase that's been around for about twenty-five years or so, and it's embraced by driver's education classes throughout the United States. Defensive driving teaches people to drive as though everyone else on the road is out to get them. The ironic thing is that some people drive as though they really are out to get you!

Knowing how to respond to hostile or aggressive drivers can keep you out of trouble, but sometimes it's not easy for us to give up our driver's ego, that force inside us that wants to retaliate for being cut off or make that tailgater pay for his or her unsafe driving habits. It's the same force that turns civilized, mild-mannered persons into cursing animals if they feel their car's space has been invaded.

Almost two out of three vehicle deaths are in rural areas.

If you can turn off your driver's ego you will be less at the mercy of unsafe drivers. And by following these tips on handling hostile drivers, you can significantly reduce your chances of an accident. Never lose sight of your goal: to get where you're going safely. Remember, these techniques may not be easy to do, but they might just save your life. Doesn't that make them worthwhile?

Tailgaters

We all hate these people. They not only invade our space, but by their rude behavior they seem to be saying, "Hey, buddy, you're driving too slow. What's wrong with you?"

The safe response: your main concern about tailgaters is that they may hit you if you have to stop fast. To avoid that situation, put some distance between you and the car in front of you. Slow down even more and move over to the right a bit and allow the tailgater to pass. (If you're in the left lane, signal and move to the right lane when it's safe.) If the tailgater won't take the hint and pass you, perhaps it's because he or she is not sure about your intentions, put your hand out and wave him or her around you. Although you're not responsible for the tailgater's safety, don't wave him or her around if there's oncoming traffic. Some traffic experts suggest that you pull off the road if you can and let the tailgaiter pass.

A Driver Who Cuts You Off

This driver really bugs us. Not only was it a dangerous move to cut us off—we could have had an accident—but this behavior shows contempt for us and our lives. We take cutting in front as one of life's snubs. Many male teenagers seem to consider cutting in front an affront to their burgeoning manhood.

The safe response: resist the temptation to retaliate. Realize that the other driver really doesn't know you, so why take it personally? Let it go. Consider yourself lucky that he or she didn't hit you.

A Slow Driver Who Won't Let You Pass

We all hate this one, don't we? If the speed limit is fifty-five, why is this guy going forty? Trucks are even worse. They seem to speed up just when we'd like to pass and slow down when we can't cross the line. *Grrrr.*

The safe response: First, make sure the driver knows you want to pass by blinking your lights or honking your horn "politely." Don't blind or deafen the slow one. He or she might just slow down and let you pass.

If a slow driver won't let you pass, or if he or she is playing cat and mouse with you, don't try to outdrive him or her. It's too dangerous. Do your best to relax and resign yourself to the fact that there's no *safe* way to go around. Pull off the road if you can. You weren't going to get where you're going faster anyway with the slowpoke in front of you. If possible, take a different route.

SAFETY BY THE NUMBERS

The most common type of motor vehicle-related deaths involves a collision between two vehicles.

A Lane-Changer Who Weaves In and Out of Traffic

Hey, what's the hurry? In your rearview mirror you see a car coming up quickly behind you, constantly changing lanes and weaving in and out of traffic.

The safe response: keep an eye on Mr. Weaver with your rearview and side mirrors. Give him plenty of opportunity to pass you. If you're in the left lane and he can go around you in the right lane, let him. If he doesn't seem to want to do that, then pull over to the right lane and let him drive by. Resist the temptation to hold him up or block him in. After all, you don't know if he's drunk or just plain nuts. One mind technique is to assume that his weaving and high-speed driving are justified. Perhaps he's trying to get to the hospital because his wife has just been admitted to the maternity ward. Also think about this: did you ever have someone weave all around only to be near you at the next traffic light? Weaving doesn't pay. It usually doesn't save any time.

If the weaver is several cars ahead of you and proceeding slowly down an open road, you start to assume the driver is drunk and you wonder whether you should pass or hang back where it's safe.

■ How to Spot a Drunk Driver ■

The National Highway Traffic Safety Administration developed this list based on results of field studies in which drunk drivers were detected. These cues are listed in descending order of probability that the person observed is driving while intoxicated. In other words, the more egregious actions are on the top.

1. Turning with wide radius.
2. Straddling center of lane marker.
3. Appearing to be drunk.
4. Almost striking an object or vehicle.
5. Weaving.
6. Driving on other than designated roadway.
7. Swerving.
8. Speed lower than ten miles per hour below the posted limit.
9. Stopping without cause in traffic lane.
10. Following too closely.
11. Drifting.
12. Tires on center lane marker.
13. Braking erratically.
14. Driving into opposing or crossing traffic.
15. Signaling inconsistent with driving actions.
16. Slow response to traffic signals (slow response, delayed start).
17. Stopping inappropriately (other than in lane).
18. Turning abruptly or illegally.
19. Accelerating or decelerating rapidly.
20. Headlights off at night.

The safe response: this is a tough call. If the slow weaver is really out of it, he might hit you if you try to pass him. On the other hand, if he's traveling very slowly, you might be able to go past him and get way ahead of him before he knows it. Driving slowly on a superhighway is dangerous for the slowpoke as well as the other drivers. The safest and most conservative response is to stay very far behind the slow driver where you can keep an eye on him and stay away from him. If you have a car phone, report this menace to the police.

Emergency!

Some automobile situations are out of your control. Here's what to do for some of the most common emergencies:

Blowouts

A blowout can cause you to lose control of your car. If the front tire blows the car will pull in the direction of the blown tire. If a rear tire goes out, the back of your car will fishtail or sway.

When either one happens, don't slam on the brakes. That will only cause your car to skid. Likewise, don't let off the gas immediately; that's almost the same as stepping on the brakes. Slow down gradually while you keep a firm grip on the wheel. Pull off to the side of the road as far as you can from traffic.

If you can get far enough off the road to safely change your tire, do so. If not, stand by your car and wait for assistance. Put your flashers on; using flares is even better.

Brake Failure

Brake failure is frightening, to say the least! Newer cars have dual brake systems that prevent such occurrences, but if you're in an older car that has a brake failure, keep pumping your brakes. You might be able to build up enough pressure to stop the car. If that doesn't work, try the parking brake. Pump it slowly because parking brakes have a tendency to grab, and that could put you into a skid. Downshift to the lowest gear to help slow the engine. If all these steps fail to slow you down, try bumping the sides of your car against some bushes, the curb, or whatever is around to help get your car stopped.

Stuck Accelerator

Accelerators have been known to stick in some particular cars, and this has been the subject of several lawsuits. Although this is a scary feeling, you must remain calm. Apply the brakes and shift into neutral. This will remove the power from your wheels. Once you do this, you should be able to coast your car to a safe place. Let other drivers know you're having a problem and are moving to the side by using your flashers and hand signals.

■ Buckle Up Wherever You Sit! ■

Every year, about five thousand backseat passengers are killed in highway accidents. Most of them would have survived had they been wearing seat belts

Seized Engine

This may happen if you've forgotten to check your oil. Without lubricant, the engine literally melts together, or "seizes." This can also occur if some other engine part malfunctions and causes the entire engine to seize. The immediate effect is a jolt. Try to remain calm and move your car over to the side of the road in neutral.

The Hood Flies Up While You're Driving

Newer cars have double hood latches, so car hoods don't fly open very often these days. However, if your hood does fly open while you're driving, bend down and look through the little crack between the hood and engine compartment. If you can't see through the crack, open the window and stick your head out to look as you work your way over to the side of the road.

Engine Fire

If your engine catches fire, pull over immediately. If you have a fire extinguisher, try to put the fire out. If the fire gets bigger move far away from the car because the gas tank may explode.

The Car "Falls Off" the Pavement

If another driver forces you off the road or if your tire slips off the edge of the pavement, your first reaction is to try to steer back onto the highway. That's fine if the shoulder is level with the pavement, but if there's a lip or a dropoff, getting back onto the road can be dangerous. You should slow down and grip the steering wheel firmly, then drive with one side of the car on the pavement and one side off until you see an opportunity to get back on the roadway safely. Wait for a break in the traffic, then steer onto the roadway and get ready to straighten out the car when the outside tire is back on the pavement.

■ Headrest Adjustment ■

One piece of automobile safety equipment that is often overlooked is the headrest. You can save yourself a severe case of whiplash or other neck injury by adjusting it so the back of your head touches the lower half of the headrest when your head tilts back. If your head touches the support post the headrest is too high. If your head misses the headrest, it's too low.

Driving at Night

Your chances of having a fatal traffic accident at night are more than three times higher than during the day. The main culprits are low visibility and fatigue. Follow these tips to reduce your risk of accident:

- Slow down. Don't overdrive your headlights. Assume there's a road hazard just past your headlights—where you can't see—and make sure you can stop in that distance.
- Don't drive when you're tired. Stop and take a nap if possible, or pack it in for the night and resume your trip in the morning.
- When dusk arrives, give your eyes a chance to adjust to the subdued light. *Night vision* sometimes takes a few minutes or longer to kick in. Don't ruin your night vision by trying to read a map under a regular lamp. Pull over and let your eyes recover. Wearing sunglasses during the day can also help your night vision, but never wear sunglasses at night.
- Use the nighttime position on your rearview mirror to reduce the glare from car headlights behind you and keep your night vision intact.
- When another car is approaching you, keep your eyes on the road ahead. Don't look directly into the headlights. If you do, it will take time for your night vision to recover.
- If you're using high beams and another car approaches, dim yours first. If the other driver doesn't follow suit, blink them a few times. If he or she still doesn't respond with low beams, don't turn on your high beams just for spite. That will make two of you with impaired vision.
- Dim your lights when you're behind another car so you don't impair the other driver's night vision.
- Never use high beams in fog. The light will reflect back and make it more difficult for you to see the road.
- If you see one headlight coming toward you in the other lane, don't assume it's a motorcycle. For safety's sake, assume it's a car with one headlight missing and drive accordingly.
- Clean your windshield inside and out. You want every

bit of light coming in. Keep your windshield washer full of cleaning fluid and make sure your wipers are free of oil and road dirt.

- Make sure your headlights are properly aimed and free of dirt. It's a good practice to clean your headlights every time you clean your windshield.

Seasonal Driving

Winter

Winter driving can be dangerous when you have hazards like ice and snow to contend with, not to mention the cold temperatures. You have no doubt seen signs that warn: "Bridge freezes before road" or "Watch for ice on bridge." Cold air circulates above and underneath bridges and helps to cool the surface faster than if the road were resting on earth. Be very careful when you're driving over a bridge any time the thermometer is near or below freezing.

SAFETY BY THE NUMBERS

More than half of all motor-vehicle deaths occur at night.

Although skidding is a problem in all kinds of weather, it's most common in winter. Skidding occurs when you brake too fast, accelerate too quickly, or turn too fast into a curve. The bottom line is that you're out of control.

If you skid because you braked too hard, the only thing you can do is let off the brakes a bit, hold the wheel straight, then pump the brakes gently. New, antilock brakes are wonderful because they do this work for you. If your skid is the result of a jackrabbit start, let off on the gas and you should be OK.

Skids in curves are a bit trickier. If you understeer in a curve, your front tires lose their grip on the road and there's nothing to stop your car from continuing to go in the direction it was heading. You're going to keep skidding. Don't add more steering. Continue to hold the wheel and aim the car in the direction you want it to go. Although it will seem like hours, in a few seconds you should have enough traction to steer normally.

When your rear wheels skid, it's called oversteering. The back of your car fishtails and could send you into a spin. Steer

The lowest motor-vehicle death rate in 1990 was in the Syrian Arab Republic, followed by Sri Lanka and Hong Kong. The United States ranked thirty-sixth.

the front wheels the same way the rear end is going. "Steer into the skid," as the saying goes. Ease off the gas. Once the car swings back, steer straight ahead. Don't steer too much or you'll fishtail in the other direction.

The proper tire can work wonders in winter, but remember, snow tires give you an advantage only on snow, not ice. Chains do give you traction on ice. So do snow tires with studs, but they're outlawed in many areas because they can ruin the pavement in non-icy weather.

Tire pressure should be set at or near the top of the recommended range because cold weather will make your tire pressure drop. Don't ever let air out of your tires thinking that more surface area will give you better traction. It may not only hurt the tires but give you poor handling, which could lead to an accident.

If you should get stuck in snow, don't accelerate your way out unless the road ahead of your car is clear and you're sure it will work on the first try. How do you know? Only experience can tell you that. For most of us, the best way to get free of snow is to rock the car back and forth by alternating between drive and reverse in a rhythm designed to move the car a little more each way with each acceleration.

Danger! If other people are helping push your car out of the snow, make sure they are not in front or behind the car. They should stand to the side of the car, away from the tires, and push.

Don't rock back and forth too long. It can hurt the transmission. Also, don't spin the tires. That doesn't get you anywhere except deeper in the snow.

It also helps to put anything you can under the tire to give you traction. Some people use pieces of carpet but this may be just as slippery as the snow once it gets wet. Carpets have also been known to shoot out with substantial force and hit people. Kitty litter works well. So do sand, chunks of salt, pebbles, and things of that nature.

Summer

More people are killed in motor vehicle accidents during the summer than the winter. Why? First, more people are on the road and second, the heat is more fatiguing to drivers. A third reason is that more people are driving for pleasure on unfamiliar roads as opposed to commuting every day on familiar highways.

Roll up your windows and use your air conditioner on very hot days. This not only keeps you cooler, but the closed windows prevent *road buzz,* that constant sound of air coming in through open windows. The noise is not that disturbing once you get used to it, but it can make you feel tired. Close the window and . . . *ah* . . . enjoy the quiet. Here are some more safety tips for summertime driving:

- Park your car in the shade whenever possible.
- Wear sunglasses to cut glare. Squinting makes you tired.
- Resist the temptation to drive barefooted. Sweaty feet can slip off pedals. Also, in an emergency you can't brake as hard without shoes.
- Although ice isn't a factor in the summer, this season is notorious for quick, out-of-nowhere rains. The main danger occurs during the first few minutes of a rain because the water brings up all the oil and gunk in the roadway. Unless the rain continues and washes it away, road surfaces can be extremely slippery. Rain also cuts down visibility. Some states have laws requiring "when the wipers go on, so do the lights." Whether or not it's the law, it's a pretty good idea to turn on your headlights in a rain shower. Don't be ashamed to pull over if the rain shower is so hard you can't see far enough to feel safe. Just be sure you're way off the road with your flashers on.
- Don't overload your car. It will not handle as safely if

you do. Don't pack the inside of the car so full that you can't see out of the rearview mirror.

- RVs and trailers travel slowly, and it's hard to see around them. Pass the big rig only if it's safe. Try not to lose your temper.
- Fatigue is dangerous. Take frequent breaks on long, summertime trips. Keep your fluids up, too, to keep yourself cooler.
- Noisy children can distract you from your driving. Take along books, personal tape recorders, and other quiet-play items to give them something to do so they won't bother you.
- Be sure your car-top carrier is tied down correctly and securely. It also must be properly balanced so it doesn't affect your steering and your ability to brake.
- There's more road construction during the summer than in the winter. Be prepared for poor-surface roads and traffic jams around work areas.

Autumn

One overlooked driving hazard of autumn is wet leaves, which can be just as slippery as any ice patch. Watch for them.

Also, be careful after the first few nights of frost. Scrape all frost from your windshield before driving, even if you're in a hurry. A "peephole" doesn't give you enough visibility to be safe.

Spring

Watch out for spring showers and don't be distracted by all the beautiful spring flowers.

Cars and Trains

One of the most common automobile accidents is caused by impatience. Despite the fact that railroad crossings are clearly marked and many have gates and signal lights, each year about five thousand motor vehicles collide with trains at railroad crossings, and hundreds of people are killed or injured.

The reason? Drivers don't want to wait for the train to pass and they think they can outrun it. All too often the driver loses the race.

It's hard to explain why drivers would risk going against a train, but it happens for several reasons.

First, drivers often think they have plenty of time before the train actually gets to them. Part of the reason is that railroad crossing lights and gates activate well in advance of the train, often before it even comes into sight. Many drivers don't want to wait because they believe the time lag is unrealistic.

Second, even when drivers see an approaching train, they don't often realize how fast the train is going because big vehicles are perceived as being slow-moving. In addition, the train tracks seem to converge in the distance—a familiar optical illusion–making the train appear farther away than it is.

> **SAFETY BY THE NUMBERS**
>
> Since 1899 almost three million people have died in the United States in motor-vehicle accidents.

The only way to prevent these accidents is to be on the conservative side. Whenever you approach a railroad crossing, slow down and take time to look both ways. This is especially important on crossings with no gates or flashing lights. At larger crossings where gates and lights warn motorists of an approaching train, when the gates go down, *stop*. Don't drive across the tracks. It's a long wait when you're in a hurry, but the consequences aren't worth the risk.

The Age Factor

When you look at the number of miles driven by different age groups and their corresponding accident rates, the rates are highest for people younger than twenty-five and older than seventy-four.

The reasons for these accident-rate "bulges" are vastly different. For people younger than twenty-five, high accident rates are usually the result of inexperience, immaturity, alcohol, or a general recklessness often found in younger people. For those older than seventy-four, the main reason is lack of mental alertness and physical ability. Let's take a closer look at the problems related to these two groups.

Teenagers

From a clinical point of view, teenagers should be the safest drivers. Their eyesight is usually excellent, their physical skills and reaction times are tops, and most likely they've recently finished an approved driver's education class.

So what gives? *Lack of experience and good judgment.*

Unfortunately, we can do little about teenagers' lack of experience; that will take time. But poor judgment may be overcome with proper discipline and education.

The deadly combination of speeding and drinking is a major factor in teen driving fatalities. So are drugs. Half of all traffic fatalities for all age groups are caused by alcohol or drug impairment, but for teenagers, that number is even higher.

Parents can help their youngsters by instituting some of the following rules. Of course, rules are always easier to make than to enforce, especially in today's environment, but parents should still insist on these minimums:

- No drinking and driving. You and your child should agree that she will telephone you for transportation if she has had too much to drink and doesn't feel sober enough to drive. Likewise, your child should not ride with a friend who has been drinking. Assure him that he can always turn down an unsafe ride and call you for transportation. Some schools have prepared statements that teens and parents can sign to make this commitment. No parent wants his or her child to drink to excess, but having the child die in a car accident is worse.
- Limit the number of passengers the child can have in

the car to three or fewer, depending upon the car. Driving a crowded car is dangerous because the driver's attention may be diverted by noise and motion.

- Teens can be very selfish and not realize the ramifications of their actions. They should know that their actions have consequences. Remind your child that reckless driving not only affects him or her but other people as well—the people in the other car or the toddler on a bike, and, of course, you, the parent.

- Always wear seat belts.

- Last, incidents of unsafe driving should result in "grounding," loss of driving privileges, or another punishment. Devise a system in which your teen and you agree that his or her negative actions will have a negative effect. Give your teenage driver full responsibility for his or her actions.

SAFETY BY THE NUMBERS

About 62 percent of Americans use seat belts. The greatest compliance is in Hawaii, which has 83 percent usage according to the National Highway Traffic Safety Administration.

The Elderly

While we tend to think of teenagers as risky drivers, people over age seventy-five drive less but have significantly higher accident rates than those of teens. At age eighty-five, accident rates jump still higher, and these drivers commit many more moving violations, such as going through stop signs and failing to yield the right of way.

Drivers who are impaired by age may try to compensate for their reduced abilities by not driving on super highways or keeping off the roads during rush hour, at night, or in inclement weather. This technique can help keep an elderly person out of harm's way, but it's often not a totally safe strategy. For example, an impaired person may not be able to avoid bad weather that crops up unexpectedly, and if he or she has not driven in a rainstorm in a long time and has forgotten the skills needed to make it a safe journey, the situation can be very dangerous.

An even more dangerous scenario is when an impaired person doesn't realize or acknowledge his or her impairment and continues to drive.

To combat this problem, some states have frequent mandatory testing for the elderly, not just when they renew their licenses, and it's very important for friends and relatives to assume responsibility for getting elderly, impaired drivers off the road for their own sake and others. In some states, physicians are required to report to the motor vehicle department any patient whose illness may hinder his safe driving. (For example, California doctors must inform the state about patients with Alzheimer's disease.) Many states simply add restrictions to an impaired person's license such as "no night driving."

A major problem for older people is poor vision caused by cataracts, glaucoma, or just the normal aging process. In addition, elderly people often don't have adequate flexibility in their neck muscles to check the full field of view while they're driving.

Another problem is medicines commonly taken by the elderly that may make them drowsy or anxious and affect their ability to make quick, correct decisions. Muscle relaxants such as Valium or Dalmane and antidepressants such as Elavil slow reaction time and impair motor skills in everyone, but their effects may be more pronounced in older people who already suffer a loss of physical and mental acuity by virtue of their age.

There have been many cases when family members take the keys away from an elderly driver who doesn't want to acknowledge his or her impairment. This is always a sad situation and often leads to friction and strife. It's always best, if possible, to convince the elderly person to give up his or her keys voluntarily before an accident occurs. Because so much of an older person's sense of self-worth may be tied to being independent, it's crucial that family members or friends make sure the unsafe driver is given a way to still get around. Carpooling is a possibility, and so are senior citizens' transportation services.

Trucks

Sharing the road with trucks isn't always easy if you're an automobile driver. Trucks are big and take up lots of space, and many truck drivers seem to be discourteous—for instance, by tailgating you until you move to another lane.

Truckers complain about cars too. They say car drivers cut in front of their trucks, not realizing that an eighty-thousand-pound vehicle can't stop in the same distance as a car. Both sides must live together on the road, no matter who is at fault. Here are some tips for sharing the road compatibly with trucks:

- Don't drive directly behind a truck in the truck driver's blind spot.
- Trucks make wide turns. Don't pass on the right if a trucker has his right turn signal on. The same goes for the left side.
- Don't assume the truck's tire splash guards will keep spray, dirt, and pebbles from hitting your windshield. Keep back.

Other Transportation

Airplanes

Giving advice about airplane safety may seem silly to some people, and let's face it: it *is* a little silly. After all, what control do you have over the plane? The pilot is flying it and you're not.

Most people take the attitude that the pilot wants to get home safely, too, and therefore will fly as carefully as possible. This is a pretty healthy tack to take, and it's true. You, as a passenger, have no control over the pilot's actions. What you do have control over, however, are a few measures you can take to increase your chances of surviving an accident or mishap if one occurs. So buckle your seat belts, put your tray tables in their upright and locked position, and let's begin.

The most important aspect of being a safe passenger is to pay attention to the cabin attendant's safety speech. Yes, I know, you've heard the spiel a hundred times before and you know what he or she is going to say. But listen anyway. If nothing else, it will get you to think about safety. Here are some of the usual highlights:

SAFETY BY THE NUMBERS

According to the National Highway Traffic Safety Administration, the leading cause of traffic accidents in cities, is running red lights; the other most common causes are hitting a vehicle from the rear, running off the road or striking an object, driving into another lane, and colliding with an oncoming vehicle.

- Note where the safety exits are. This is the most important piece of information you can acquire. Count the number of rows to the nearest exit so you can find it more easily during an emergency. And remember that in some cases the nearest exit is *behind* you.
- During takeoff and landing, store packages and luggage under the seat in front of you and in the overhead bin. If an emergency occurs, you may not have time to get it out of your way.
- Know what to do if the oxygen mask falls down. It's crucial that you place it over your face first and then a child's.
- Although children under certain ages can sit on your lap for free, buy them a ticket and bring along an approved car seat. If there's an accident, this will enhance their chances of survival. Also, car seats should be by the window and not the aisle because they're sometimes difficult to get past on your way to the aisle.
- Always wear your seat belt when you're in your seat.
- All domestic U.S. flights are nonsmoking—and this includes the lavatory.

Here are some additional tips for maximizing your chances to survive an airplane emergency:

- Never wear earphones during takeoff and landing. You may not hear emergency instructions.
- Open the window shade during takeoff and landing. Knowing something is wrong a few seconds before an emergency occurs may help you prepare for it.
- Statistics about fatalities and which part of the plane people sit in, such as over the wing or in the rear, have largely been debunked. It doesn't matter much where you sit, except that sitting in the row with the exit might enhance your chances of a quick escape depending upon how the plane rests on the ground after a crash.

Cruise Ships

Ships registered in the United States must meet Coast Guard safety regulations and be inspected annually. Ships registered outside the United States (which includes almost all of the world's cruise ships) must meet international regulations set forth in 1974 if they are to take on passengers at U.S. ports.

To ensure compliance of all ships, even those registered outside the U.S., the Coast Guard examines the ship when it goes into service at a U.S. port and checks it every quarter. Records of these examinations are public record and you can get them from the Coast Guard. Ask for Control Verification Examination results. The Coast Guard's consumer hot line is 800–368-5647. The Coast Guard also checks that all crew members are properly licensed for their specific jobs.

On voyages lasting more than a week, the Coast Guard requires that an emergency drill be held before the ship leaves port, so if you board late you may miss it. Additional drills must be held at least once a week during the cruise. On voyages of one week or less, the drills must be held within twenty-four hours of leaving port.

Pay careful attention to the notice, which is required to be posted in your cabin, that explains the ship's emergency alarm bells and whistle signals, the location of life preservers and how to put them on, and the location of the lifeboat to which you've been assigned. Direction signs pointing to life-boats are also posted throughout the ship.

The U.S. Public Health Service is responsible for oversight of cruise ships' sanitation, including water quality, food storage, handling, and preparation, and general cleanliness. The results of surprise and scheduled inspections are public record. To find out how your ship scored on these inspections contact the Vessel Sanitation Program, Centers for Disease Control, 1015 North American Way, Room 107, Miami, Florida 33132, telephone 305–536-4307. The program's "Green Sheet" compares scores for all inspected ships, or you can get a full report on the ship you're sailing on.

There are no requirements a cruise ship must meet when it comes to health and medical care. In fact, the Coast Guard regulations don't require that a ship carry a doctor, even though all ships routinely have medical staffs on board. If medical attention is of importance to you, check with the cruise line about the ship's health-care facilities before you travel.

CHAPTER 5

Peace of Mind in the City or on the Town

WHEN WE LOOK at safety and health issues, we must look, sadly, at crime and violence.

Unfortunately, violence has become an integral part of the fabric of American life (some say it's always been there), and clearly it's becoming more pronounced and more aggressive every year. Crime used to be the concern primarily of those who lived in cities, but now it has spread to suburbia and even to more rural areas. None of us are immune from crime's reach no matter where we live or what we do for a living.

This chapter will discuss only crimes against people. Having your car stolen while it's parked at the mall is a terrible thing, but it won't hurt you—at least not physically. You may cry and be angry, but you won't be injured. We'll focus on the crimes that affect your health and well-being.

Home Burglary Protection

Although "crimes against property," as the FBI calls them, don't usually involve violence against people, you may become a victim if you're in the area or try to intercede. Home burglary is a good example. The burglar's intention isn't to hurt you; it's to take your stuff. If you're around, however, you could be injured.

Fifty-five percent of all crimes committed are larcenies. Other crime percentages are burglary, 21 percent; car theft, 11 percent; assault, 7 percent; robbery, 5 percent; rape, 1 percent; and murder, less than .2 percent. Statistics provided by the F.B.I.

Protecting your home doesn't require any complicated procedures. You need only institute some simple but effective measures to vastly increase your security. The main theory behind house protection is this: most burglars don't want to spend a lot of time breaking into a house. If they can't do it quickly, they'll move on. That's why burglar alarms are effective. It's easier and safer for the burglar to bypass a house with a burglar alarm for one that doesn't have such protection. This statement has been proven time and again during interviews with career burglars.

So your goal isn't to make your house impenetrable. That's virtually impossible unless you live in a castle with a moat and armed guards. Instead, your aim is to make it difficult and time-consuming for a burglar to enter your house.

Let's look at the simple measures you can take to make your house less desirable to burglars.

Doors

Burglars in the movies pick locks. Real-life burglars try to yank them out of the door with crowbars. So one of your best defenses against burglars is a strong, solid door with a deadbolt lock. Sounds simple doesn't it? Yet every day homes are broken into by burglars who simply smash open a flimsy back door. (We tend to pay more attention to our front doors than our back doors, which is a mistake.) Your door should be several inches thick and *solid,* not hollow like the doors between rooms inside your house.

Most robberies occur during October and December. The fewest occur in April according to the F.B.I.

Always install deadbolt locks, never spring-operated locks, on outside doors. The hardware that holds the lock to the door should be made of steel (brass is too soft) and embedded at least two to three inches inside the wood. The bolt from the lock should fit snugly into the doorjamb plate. This plate should be screwed into the door-jamb with steel screws that are several inches long.

Burglars often jimmy the door open by prying the door-jamb away from the wall of the entrance way, so make sure the doorjamb is secured to the frame with long nails or screws. You can have the best lock in the world, but it won't do any good if the doorjamb is easily pried from the frame.

■ Dogs ■

When experienced burglars were asked what single factor deterred them from burglarizing a house or apartment, the overwhelming majority said the same thing: The presence of a dog.

If there's a window in your door, make sure it can't be broken to allow someone to slip a wire (or a hand) through it and open the lock. Back the window with a wire mesh, a thin grate, or acrylic plastic to prevent it from being used as a way inside.

Take the same precaution with your mail slot. Test it to see if you can put your hand through and open the lock.

Sliding Glass Doors

Burglars have a relatively easy entry point into a home with sliding glass doors because these doors can be lifted right out of their frame by anyone who knows how to do it.

The solution is simple, though. Place spacers or screws with big heads in the groove. This will keep the "play" space to a minimum and prevent the door from being lifted. At the same time, you should put a bar or piece of wood inside the door in the groove. This will keep the door from being opened at all. You can buy bars with locks on them specially made for sliding glass doors.

Also, check the locks on these doors. Because the doors are usually aluminum, the lock bolts tend to wear away the soft metal's doorjamb plate. You think you're locking it when all the bolt is holding is air. Again, don't rely on these locks alone for security.

Windows

Low windows offer burglars strong potential entry points. The latches that come on many windows are useless for security purposes; it's too easy to break the window and open the latch. Instead, on all windows, even high windows, install locks that must be opened with keys. Keep the key handy at the side of the window in case of fire.

A good alternative is to drill a hole in the window frame and insert a long, thick, headless nail. The nail should not stick out of the hole; you should use tweezers to remove it.

If you'd like to keep the window open a few inches for air, you can drill a hole in the frame a few inches up. This will allow you to open the window and insert the nail in the hole for safety. But remember, an open window loses much of its structural integrity and is then subject to prying and ripping away from the wall by a burglar with a pry bar.

You can buy locks for crank-type or jalousie windows too. It's a good practice to remove the crank handle and keep it away from the window but in a handy spot.

In high-crime areas, many people bolt bars to their window frames. This a very effective deterrent, but it can be a problem if you must exit quickly because of a fire. Instead, install gates that swing open to the outside and keep the key nearby.

Alarms

There is little doubt about it: burglar alarms deter burglars. According to the National Burglar and Fire Alarm Association, burglars target premises without alarms two to six times more often than those with alarms.

However, the first thing you should realize is that no burglar alarm can or should take the place of a secure environment. The best alarm system in the world is no substitute for a strong door with a deadbolt lock. Likewise, a burglar alarm is never a replacement for a window with a broken lock. You should also be aware that no burglar-alarm system is 100 percent foolproof. Although most systems will thwart unskilled burglars, no system can guarantee absolute protection against a determined, skilled, professional housebreaker.

With that said, if you want to get a burglar alarm system, there are many factors to consider. The first is whether or not you want to install the system yourself or have an alarm company do it. Alarm systems are not as tricky as some alarm installation companies would have you believe. On the other hand, it's not easy unless you have had some experience with wiring and electronics. Many alarm kits come with instructions that allow you to do a professional-quality job if you have the proper skills and tools.

The main reason for buying a do-it-yourself system is price. The cost of the components is roughly the same whether you install your own or have it installed. By doing it yourself, your saving labor costs.

There are advantages, however, in spending the extra money for a professional installation. First, the major cause of false alarms and alarms failing to go off when tripped is poor installation. This can lead to irate neighbors awakened by a blaring siren or a police department that may fine you when its officers have to respond to false alarms.

Probably the prime reason for going with professional installers is that these systems are usually monitored twenty-four hours a day at a central station. If this is the kind of protection you desire, a professional installation is the only way to go. As a rule, security companies will not respond to alarm systems they have not installed or had contracted to their standards.

■ Decal or No Decal? ■

One of the most controversial topics in the alarm industry is whether to place a decal on your windows or a small sign in your yard warning would-be intruders that the building is protected by a security system.

Some say it acts as a deterrent. Others believe it does the opposite by letting professional burglars, who know the idiosyncrasies of how one company installs its systems, take advantage of that knowledge. They also say that an alarmed house gives the impression that there is something worth stealing inside and that burglars may try a quick break-in in the hopes that the alarm will be off or not operating that day.

Another aspect to consider is that so many people buy phony stickers to place on windows that some burglars disregard decals and take their chances anyway.

So, should you warn would-be burglars that you have an alarm? Most experts say yes. The majority of burglars are amateurs and will either be stopped or deterred very quickly by an alarm. Burglary is clearly a crime of opportunity, and most burglars would prefer to go after a house without an alarm system.

The first line of defense against intruders is called *perimeter protection*. It senses burglars before they actually enter the premises. For example, a detector on a window that sounds an alarm when the window is broken is considered a perimeter alarm.

The second defense is known as *area protection*. This sounds an alarm when someone is actually in the house. A good example is a sensor under a mat in front of the master bedroom.

While some people install only perimeter or only area protection, your best defense is to install both. Ideally, you want an intruder detected before he or she enters your home. This is the safest scenario for anyone inside. The area alarm should be thought of as a backup to the perimeter alarm, to scare the intruder out of the interior area if he or she should breach the perimeter system.

Many kinds of sensors and detectors are used on windows and doors depending on the level of protection you want and the layout of the house. The best all-around protection, however, is probably afforded by an *audio sensor* connected to an alarm company. This device is a very sensitive microphone tuned to respond to noises such as breaking glass or a door being forced open. The installer has to set the sensitivity, and that can be tricky if you live on a busy street because outside noises such as trucks or buses can trigger the alarm.

One of the benefits of audio sensors is that once they are triggered, the security company attendant can employ them to listen to activities in the house. If the attendant determines that a noise was caused by a break-in, and not something else (such as a truck backfiring), he or she will contact the police. In a sense, the audio sensor combines the best attributes of a perimeter and area sensor.

Other Ways to Increase Your Home Security

- Skylights should be made of shatter-resistant plastic and have locking mechanisms.
- Keep all shrubs and bushes trimmed so a burglar can't hide while he or she is trying to open your windows. Shrubs afford an excellent opportunity for a burglar to work at gaining entry over several nights in a row before he or she actually breaks in.
- Lights are a strong deterrent to burglars. Motion detectors that turn on outside lights when someone walks in your backyard are scary to burglars. Keep porch lights on all night.
- Never leave anything of value, such as a purse or wallet, in full view of your window. It's too tempting for a

burglar to smash the window and grab the item. He could have your purse in hand before the first shard of glass hits the floor.

- Never leave anything in your yard that a burglar can use to enter your house such as a ladder, hammer, crowbar, or piece of lumber that can be thrown through a window.

- Don't hide your house keys in obvious places such as under the doormat or over the door frame. If you want to leave a spare key outside the house for emergencies, bury it in your yard under a few inches of soil. If you're locked out, a few minutes and dirty hands won't make a big difference to you, but it will keep the key away from a potential burglar. (Wrap the key in paper towels to absorb moisture and place it in plastic bag. Not only will it keep the key rust-free for a long while but it will be easier to find.) Some people buy make-believe rocks that hold keys inside and leave them in the garden, but many burglars know what these pseudo-rocks look like.

The Human Component to Home Security

The previous sections dealt with the physical side of burglary prevention—doors, locks, alarms, and other structural aspects of your home. But there's a human component to all of this too. Here are some personal tips for keeping your home safe and secure:

- Never open the door to anyone unless you know who it is.
- Know all your neighbors. Everyone should watch everyone else's house.
- If you go away for an extended time, let your neighbors know about it. Have them take in newspapers, mail, and anything else that indicates an empty home. Arrange for your grass to be cut.
- Never leave notes on your door saying you're out and specifying when you'll return.
- Consider automatic timers to turn lights on and off.

The best ones activate lights at slightly different times each day.

- Don't leave a message on your answering machine that says you're out of town.
- Most police departments offer free security checks of homes. They will tell you if your home has any weak security points.
- Join the Neighborhood Watch program or start one with the assistance of the local police.
- Immediately report all suspicious persons in your neighborhood to the police. Police would much rather challenge a suspicious person than respond to a crime scene. Foster a reputation that your neighborhood is one in which residents get involved and will not tolerate crime. Criminals know which neighborhoods call the police and which do not.

Apartment Living

Many of the preceding suggestions for burglar-proofing your home, such as those recommending strong doors and locks on the windows, also apply to an apartment or condominium. Apartment dwellers, though, have additional considerations that must be addressed.

SAFETY BY THE NUMBERS

According to F.B.I. statistics, the safest region the United States is the Midwest; the most dangerous areas are in the West.

Before you move into an apartment or condo, make sure the front door to the building is strong and secure and closes behind you when you enter and locks automatically. The buzzer-intercom system should work properly so you don't buzz someone in who doesn't belong in the building.

If there's a security guard, make sure he or she knows what the residents expect in the way of screening visitors.

If your apartment building has outside fire escapes, pay special attention to the locks on windows that have access to the fire escape. They should be secure yet easily opened from the inside in case of fire.

If your building has inside fire stairs, make sure the doors are locked from the stairs side on all floors except the ground floor or basement (whatever the fire code specifies). This will cut down on intruders hiding in the stairwells.

Know all your neighbors and watch out for each other. If you hear someone pressing all the buzzers or doorbells, call the police. Few buildings these days allow solicitors free access to roam the building.

SAFETY BY THE NUMBERS

The most common place for a robbery is in the street. The least likely place to be robbed is in a bank. Statistic provided by the F.B.I.

Make sure all common areas such as parking lots, laundry rooms, hallways, and basements are secure and well lighted. Encourage all residents to periodically check the security of common-area doors, locks, and windows.

If you're a renter, know your rights to a safe and secure building. Learn what security measures the landlord is required to provide. If you're a condominium owner, convey to the management company through the condominium association, or whatever group the owners have formed, that security is a priority.

Muggings

One of the scariest violent crimes is a mugging. Sometimes it involves brandished weapons, but often just the threat of bodily harm from a stranger is enough to terrorize the victim.

Law enforcement officials suggest that when you're confronted by a would-be mugger you should give up your possessions readily. In the majority of cases you'll lose your wallet or purse but keep your life.

The best way to keep from being a mugging victim is to

be alert and aware of your surroundings. Keep away from alleys, empty side streets, and deserted areas.

The most violent "state" in the United States according to F.B.I. data, measured by per capita crime, is the District of Columbia. The lowest is North Dakota.

Know where you're walking and carry yourself with confidence. Muggers have "victim radar" that identifies people who look vulnerable. This is not to suggest that victims are to blame or that it's your fault if you're mugged. However, anecdotal evidence suggests that muggers would much rather approach someone they think they can intimidate instead of someone who looks like they might resist. Always walk confidently and with purpose. Hold your head high and look and act like you know what's going on around you. Convey that sense to those around you.

■ Crimes against the Elderly ■

Many elderly persons are particularly vulnerable to violent crime. They can increase their chances of staying safe by following these suggestions:

- Have all your regular checks, such as Social Security, pension, etc., directly deposited to your bank account. Many muggers are most active during the first few days of the month when they can rob elderly people of their Social Security checks.
- Don't give any personal information over the phone to strangers. A potential burglar might call and pose as a pollster doing a survey. He might be tempted to rob you based on what he learns about your financial situation.
- Never open the door to strangers no matter who they say are. If you live in an apartment, check with the management office before admitting repair workers or others who knock on your door unexpectedly.
- Be alert to potential muggers walking behind you who could push you to the ground to get your purse or wallet. Hold your purse close to your body to prevent someone from running by and grabbing the strap. Or better yet, don't carry a purse at all.

Men should carry their wallets in an inside pocket instead of letting it bulge out of a hip pocket.

- Elderly people are often victims of *push-ins,* where a mugger follows them to their door and as soon as they open it, he pushes inside. If someone is following you, don't go home. Head for a safe haven such as a store or public building and call the police.
- Try to do errands with other people. Lone, elderly persons are prime prey for muggers.
- Always report crimes. In most cities, areas with more reported crimes receive increased police presence.
- Don't make yourself a target by calling attention to the amount of money you're carrying. For example, count your money while you're still at the teller's window in the bank, not as you walk out.
- Don't overload your arms with packages; this makes you vulnerable. Likewise, don't call attention to yourself by wearing expensive jewelry in unsafe neighborhoods.
- Whenever possible, travel with other people.
- Trust your instincts about your surroundings. If you feel you're being followed or eyed by someone, you're probably right. If you feel uncomfortable in an area or a situation, leave immediately.

Should You Resist?

This is one of those questions that has no blanket answer for all situations. In the majority of cases, you're going to be better off if you give the mugger what he or she wants. On the other hand, if you're threatened with bodily harm and giving up your possessions doesn't seem to alleviate the mugger's wish to harm you, then resisting may be beneficial.

Muggers are bullies and don't want attention from other people. If you shout and scream you may scare the mugger away or bring other people to the scene.

Many people have taken personal defense courses and used it successfully. Others have tried to use what they learned and it only prolonged dangerous contact with their aggressor. The only answer is to take each situation individually and handle it the way you think will be safest for you.

Chemical self-defense weapons have become quite popular these days. Again, some people have used them successfully while others have made the situation worse for themselves. Still others ended up worse for the effort but felt better emotionally about fighting back. It's for you to decide. If you decide to carry a chemical spray, most law enforcement officials now use and recommend pepper-based products instead of conventional tear gas gadgets. You'll see pepper-based sprays called *OC* gas, which stands for *oleoresin-capsicum.* Be aware that OC and some other products are illegal in some states.

A pepper-based spray causes an immediate swelling of surface capillaries. If it gets in the attacker's eyes, he or she involuntarily closes them. If inhaled, OC causes swelling of the respiratory membranes and breathing becomes difficult. The attacker is immobilized and in great pain. The effect is temporary and lasts about a half-hour, certainly long enough to get away from the scene.

Rape

One of the most horrendous crimes, rape, is increasing in incidence. According to researchers, most rapes are planned. The rapist selects his victim ahead of time, follows her, and waits for the right opportunity to attack. The whole act from stalking to actually committing the rape could take only a few minutes or it could take several days or weeks.

Because of this time factor, women sometimes have the opportunity to keep out of harm's way. Always keep your guard up, especially if you're traveling alone, It's certainly not the most pleasant way to live—with your guard up all the time—but constant alertness has become a necessary fact of life in our society.

SAFETY BY THE NUMBERS

Most rapes occur during August. The fewest occur in December, according to the F.B.I.

Trust your instincts. Many rape victims felt something was wrong before the attack but didn't trust their gut feeling or decided to override it in an attempt to believe they were just being paranoid. Some women said they didn't want to hurt a stranger's feelings by not getting on the elevator with him.

If a situation doesn't feel right, do something about it. Run away, yell, or do whatever it takes for you to be comfortable and in control.

Develop safe habits. Always lock your car doors as soon as you get inside. The same goes for your house; lock the doors immediately once you've entered.

Be careful when giving your phone number or address to a sales clerk when other people are around. Offer to write it down for the clerk or whisper it over the counter.

One of the most controversial issues concerning rape prevention is clothing. Does a woman who dresses in a sexy fashion invite rape? To believe prosecutors in rape trials the answer is no, but to hear defense attorneys tell it, the answer may be yes. The truth is that rape is not a sexual crime. It's a crime of violence and opportunity and, according to studies, the way in which a women dresses may affect her chance of being raped. A woman who dresses in an alluring manner may—to the twisted mind of a sex offender—look more vulnerable than if she were dressed in a different way. In addition, rapists know that women in stylish high heels or tight clothing can't run away as easily as a women wearing flats and a loose dress or slacks.

The issue of fighting a rapist becomes even more heated than the issue of fighting a mugger. Studies are inconclusive as to whether a woman is better off resisting a rapist or whether submitting to the attack will save her life. Some studies suggest that women who resist end up better, while other studies show the opposite. Again, it comes down to each victim, each rapist, and each situation. Sometimes a would-be attacker will back off when confronted with resistance. Sometimes it will only spur him on. There's no way of knowing which way it will work out. Each woman has to make her own decision when the time comes.

It's highly recommended that women take rape-prevention classes, which offer the latest techniques on avoiding attacks. They also give women an air of confidence that can help keep them from becoming a victim.

Automatic Teller Machines

Getting money from an automatic teller machine, or ATM, is a convenience, but it also supplies criminals with a new way to rob you. Don't use ATMs that are in dark or remote areas. If you're alone and someone suspicious approaches you while you're at the ATM, leave immediately. Don't finish your transaction. Leave your card in the machine if necessary but leave in a hurry. ATM withdrawals have limits, usually a few hundred dollars, and it's not worth losing your life over it. You can always come back later and retrieve your card or call the bank in the morning and tell them what happened.

If someone approaches you and demands that you withdraw money from the machine, do it. There are limits to how much can be taken out during a twenty-four-hour period, and it's not worth fighting over.

Some criminals have added a new, nefarious twist to ATM robberies. They carjack you and make you drive to an ATM to withdraw money. If this happens, what do you do?

First, remain calm. Criminals are jumpy people and may be on drugs or alcohol. The calmer you can remain, the cooler the robber will be. Don't try to reason or argue with the person. Just ask what he or she wants and say you will comply. Your goal is to get out of the situation unharmed. will be. Don't try to reason or argue with the person. Just ask what he or she wants and say you will comply. Your goal is to get out of the situation unharmed.

Experts differ on whether you should try to escape or not. It's similar to a mugging or rape situation. Stay alert for chances to escape, and if you think you can escape without further danger, do so. If you can jump out of your car at the stop light, especially if there are lots of people around, do it. However, if you believe you would be hurt by trying to escape, stay put and follow the robber's instructions. Your only other alternative is to hope that the robber leaves you alone after he or she gets the money.

Carjacking

Americans love their automobiles. Cars represent freedom and privacy—especially privacy. For some people, the only time they have any time to themselves is when they're driving. That's one reason why carjacking terrifies us. Not only is it a dangerous, violent crime, but it strikes us where we think we're safe—inside our cars.

Carjacking is not really a new crime. Criminals have been stealing cars at gunpoint since cars were invented, but it's increased in the past few years at an alarming rate. In 1991, about twenty thousand carjackings occurred. To many criminals, strong-arming a car is easier than stealing an unattended vehicle. You don't have to waste time fiddling with door and ignition locks, and there's no alarm to disable.

The Most Common ■ Times for Carjacking ■

Most carjackings occur between 10 P.M. and 2 A.M., although midmorning carjackings are becoming more commonplace. Fridays and Saturdays are also prime carjacking times. Carjackers prefer times when the roads are uncrowded.

There doesn't seem to be any particular pattern or typical carjacking victim, although police report that women are victims more often than men. People who drive alone are more apt to be carjacked. Protecting yourself from a carjacking is tough, but there are some things you can do to lessen your chances of becoming a victim:

- Always keep your windows closed and your doors locked.
- Be aware that many carjackings take place at stoplights where the attacker runs up to the stopped car and opens the door. What should you do if a carjacker holds a gun to the closed window in an attempt to get you to open the door? That's a tough call. Clearly, your

life is more important than your car, but you also may be able to step on the gas and drive away before he or she can open the door.

- When you're entering your car, get in as quickly as possible and lock the doors. Don't fumble for your keys. Have them ready as you approach the car.
- Carjackings often occur when drivers are leaving their cars. Look around before you turn off the engine and open the door.
- Be alert to your surroundings, especially at stoplights and stop signs. Don't get too close to the car in front of you in case you need to pull out in a hurry to escape someone who's approaching your car.
- Any car can be a target of carjackings, not just expensive ones.
- Be wary of large parking lots where you have to park far away from the building. Parking lots near freeways are prime spots for carjackers because they have quick, easy access to high-speed roads to get them away from the scene.
- Gas stations are also very fruitful spots for carjackers. Be very careful when filling up your tank, especially at night.

Carjackers also use a technique known as *bump-and-rob*. Here's how it happens: A car will hit you from behind. The driver steps out as if he is going to assess the damage and exchange license information. Instead, he robs you or takes your car. He may have an accomplice in the other car so he can drive your car away.

The best advice if you're hit is to remain calm but alert. If you're suspicious of the person in the other car—and there's nobody else around—wave to indicate that the other driver should follow you and move to a nearby spot where there are people. If it's a legitimate accident, you can explain your leaving the scene later. In fact, contrary to popular belief, most states don't require you to stay at the scene of a *minor* accident until the police arrive.

If the other driver doesn't follow you away from the scene or if you lose each other, you can fulfill your legal obligation by going to the nearest phone and calling the police to report the accident. Tell them you were afraid to get out of your car.

Bogus Police Officers

This brings us to another type of crime that is not rampant but is occurring more frequently: people posing as police officers in unmarked cars, pulling motorists over and robbing or assaulting them. All it takes is an official-looking badge and a portable blue or red flashing light in the front windshield of a car to make innocent victims believe the person waving them over is a police officer.

Again, if you have any doubt about the authenticity of the person who pulled you over, acknowledge him or her with a wave, then drive directly—at a reasonable speed—to an inhabited area before you let the person approach your car.

Police in unmarked cars who pull motorists over for traffic infractions almost always wear uniforms. If the person approaching your car isn't in uniform, you have every reason to be concerned.

Away from Home

Travelers are prime targets for criminals because they are in a strange place and may not know where to walk or drive to reach safety. But there are steps you can take to make yourself less vulnerable.

Airports

Airports are usually safe places because of all the people around, but they also represent crime hazards that are not found elsewhere. Airport travelers should be alert at all times.

This wariness is especially important in airport parking

lots, which are often huge. Park as close to the tollbooth or terminal as you can to limit your exposure. If possible, leave your bags at the terminal while you get your car. This will leave you unburdened and make you less of a target for a mugger. Conversely, drop your bags at the terminal before you park your car if possible so you can have your keys ready, in your hand, before you reach your car.

Never leave valuables in your car and always take your parking ticket with you on the plane. This will cut down on the chances of someone stealing your car for the price of the parking fee. If you have two cars, take the older one to be parked in the lot. Or take a cab to the airport instead of your car. This might even be cheaper for long trips. In fact, if your car is way out on a remote lot, you might consider taking a cab from the terminal to your car.

SAFETY BY THE NUMBERS

Based on all crimes committed, the "state" with the highest crime rate per capita, according to the F.B.I., is the District of Columbia. The lowest is West Virginia.

Very few people have reasons to hang out in airport parking lots. Be suspicious of anyone sitting in a car parked in an airport lot.

If you need to take a cab from the airport, go to the designated taxi stand. Don't take a cab that solicits you from any other area. Be wary of limo drivers who say they have just dropped off the boss and are "deadheading" back home. They're probably just trying to make a few bucks for themselves and the last thing they want is to mess up their employer's car, but you should avoid them anyway. If they're ripping off their boss, they could rip you off as well.

Hotel Safety

Hotel guests are prime targets for thieves. Vacationers often let down their guard in an attempt to relax. In addition, they have no idea whether or not their hotel or motel room has been designed with safety in mind. There have been some recent court cases in which budget-priced hotels have been sued by guests who were assaulted in their rooms because of poor hotel security. In most cases, the guests won a judgment or settled for compensation. Although most hotels and motels take appropriate security measures to ensure their guests' have a safe visit, it's still up to you to take charge of your own safety.

Trust your instincts. If the hotel lobby makes you feel unsafe or creepy when you arrive, don't check in. Sometimes, if you're stuck in the middle of nowhere, you may not have a choice of accommodations. Then you'll have to decide for yourself if you'd rather drive a little farther or stay in a motel that doesn't feel right.

Always survey the room before you check in. Many hotels and motels allow you to do this or they permit you to change rooms if you're not satisfied. **If there is anything unsafe about the room—the door is damaged, the lock doesn't lock correctly, the window doesn't close and lock—inform the management immediately and ask to change rooms.**

Close the door every time you enter. Use the double lock when you're inside.

Don't open the door for anyone you don't know. If the caller says "room service" and you didn't order anything, call the front desk. You don't want to turn away a bona fide complimentary gift, but you don't want to let a robber in either. Check the locks on all sliding glass doors and the doors connected to adjoining rooms.

Place all your valuables in the hotel vault. Don't carry them around, and don't try to hide them in your room. Carry travelers checks and keep cash to a minimum. Keep a copy of the check numbers separate from the checks. Don't show large amounts of cash in public areas such as the lobby. When you check out, wait until you are at the desk to open your wallet or purse. Report any suspicious people in or around the hotel to the management.

Pay attention to any safety material the management has placed in your room. Ask at the desk if there have been any problems recently either in the hotel or in the neighborhood. Before you go out for fresh air or a jog, ask the desk clerk or concierge if there are any areas you should avoid.

Never meet strangers, for example, business clients, in your room. Meet them in the lobby, bar, or restaurant.

Don't display your room key in public areas or leave it on your restaurant table. When telling the restaurant to what room to charge the bill, do it out of earshot of other people—or write it down for the waiter when you sign the bill.

Fire Safety in Hotels. Hotel fires have received a great deal of attention in recent years because result of some devastating fires in high-rise hotels. Here are some suggestions for keeping yourself safe in case of a fire:

- When you make a reservation, ask if the hotel or motel has automatic sprinklers and smoke detectors. The overwhelming majority of facilities do, but a few may not because older fire codes are in force.
- When you arrive, read the fire-safety information, which is usually on the back of your room door. The sign should tell you where the nearest first exit is. Take a walk down the hall and check it out. Pay attention to the floor because that's where you'll be crawling during a fire emergency. Some people even count the number of doors to the exit so they can find it in the dark.
- Locate the fire alarm on your floor. If it's a "local" alarm that sounds only in the building, the fire department will have to be notified separately.
- If a fire starts in your room, get out immediately and notify the fire department. If it's in the hall, touch your door to check for heat. If it's cool, open it slowly and head for the nearest exit. **Take your key with you.** If your escape route is blocked, the safest place is back inside your room. Crawl low to the floor where the air is less smoky. A wet towel over your face will help you breathe. When you reach the fire stairs, grab the handrail and walk down. If you encounter smoke, climb back upstairs.
- Never use elevators in a fire.

- If the door is hot, don't open it. Stay inside and stuff wet towels under the door to keep smoke out. Shut off fans and air conditioners.
- Use the phone to call for help.
- Wave at the window or hold up sheets to let fire fighters know you're trapped. Open the window a little bit at the top or bottom to let some fresh air in, but be prepared to close it if smoke enters your room. The one exception to this rule is if you can jump out of the window to the street without injuring yourself.

■ What's behind the numbers? ■

Statistics can be helpful in helping you decide where to travel, where not to travel, and how to handle yourself when you get there, but statistics don't tell the whole story. For example, Miami has one of the highest homicide rates per capita compared with other cities its size, according to the FBI's Uniform Crime Reports. However, Miamians say that the population figure used for the comparison should include visitors from around the world who swell the city's numbers all year. If you include these people in the population, they say, the per capita crime figure would be low.

In another example, Burlington, Vermont, in a beautiful rural area, has one of the lowest per capita violent crime rates in the nation, but property crimes are high because of off-season break-ins of vacant vacation homes. Therefore, Burlington's overall crime rate is high for its small population. When you look at the FBI crime rates for Burlington, you'd think it was one of the most dangerous cities in America. So always probe beyond the statistics to see what's behind the numbers.

Statistically, more crime occurs in big cities than in small towns, yet some people live their entire lives in metropolitan areas without ever becoming crime victims while some small-town residents may have been mugged several times.

The important thing is knowing how to avoid becoming a crime victim. Those who know about crime prevention lower their chances of becoming victims. That's 100 percent certain.

Car Safety When You Travel

Vacationers' cars are prime targets for robbers. Don't leave anything valuable in your car. Take your things inside with you.

If possible, don't drive rental cars that are clearly marked as such. Rental car decals, stickers, and license-plate holders may make you more vulnerable to crime by telling would-be robbers you're from out of town. In some resort cities, renters may request rental cars with no rental-company stickers or markings and no indication on the license plate that it's a rental.

Foreign Travel

Compared with citizens in other countries, we Americans travel relatively little outside of our own country. People raised in Europe, on the other hand, have usually been to many other countries by the time they've reached their teens. One reason for this difference is that Americans are somewhat isolated, geographically, from most other countries. In addition, the United States is so large that many Americans have chosen to "see America first" before heading overseas. As a result, many Americans aren't well versed in the vagaries of foreign travel that have become second nature to people in some countries.

Before traveling overseas, check with the U.S. State Department to see if it has issued a *travel advisory* for the country you're planning to visit. These advisories warn you of possible dangers from terrorism, civil unrest, disease, and other problems. This doesn't mean you're not allowed to visit. It's simply a mechanism for alerting you to potential hazards before you leave the United States. (The State Department does have a list of countries to which Americans, except those exempt under certain rules, are prohibited to travel. Cuba is one example.) Very often, a travel advisory only applies to part of a country and not the whole nation.

The State Department and Public Health Service will also advise you what inoculations, if any, you'll need to get before you enter a foreign country. The goal is to prevent you from contracting a disease in a foreign land and then bringing it back home. Some foreign countries have their own requirements for vaccinations, too, before a foreigner may enter. Before you go, learn about the places you plan to visit by reading travel guides. The State Department also publishes country guides for individual countries. In addition:

- Familiarize yourself with local laws and customs. You don't have to study all the country's laws, but you should, for example, know if it prohibits alcohol consumption.
- Keep up-to-date on recent political developments.
- Carry a copy of the prescription necessary medicines, including the generic names of the drugs. If any medications contain narcotics, carry with you a letter from your physician attesting to your need to take the drug.
- Take an extra pair of eyeglasses as well as the eyeglass prescription.
- Make copies of your airline tickets, passport, driver's license, travelers check numbers, and your credit cards. Leave one set with someone at home and carry one set with you. Also give that person a copy of your itinerary. If you're ill or traveling in areas of medical danger, it's also a good idea to give the person back home a copy of medical records so a foreign doctor can access them quickly if necessary.
- If you're concerned about safety, stay in larger hotels. They usually have better security.
- Despite what you see in old movies, being an American citizen and making a single call to the U.S. embassy does not always get you out of hot water with local authorities. Before you engage in any questionable behavior, check the local laws. Activities that are minor infractions in the United States may be of major consequence in another country.
- Never exchange money on the black market. Deal only with authorized agents.
- In some countries, it's illegal to take photos of police officers, buildings, airports, and military personnel. Always ask if you may take a photo. This holds true

for people you see in the street. Although it may not be illegal to take pictures of people, it could get you in big trouble.

- Learn a few phrases in the local language so you can get help from a doctor or the police.

High-Risk Travel

If you're going on vacation, you're probably not going to venture into a high-risk area. At least not on purpose. But if you're traveling on business or some other reason compels you to enter unstable areas, you should heed the following advice:

- Keep abreast of potential political or military problems. If you're not sure of an area, check in and register with the nearest U.S. embassy or consulate. Ask for the American Citizens Service Unit in the consular section.
- Be cautious about discussing personal matters, your itinerary, or other travel plans with strangers.
- Don't leave any personal or business papers in your hotel room.
- Be wary of people following you or watching your activities.
- Note safe areas such as police stations, hotels, hospitals, and embassies.
- Tell a trusted person about your travel plans, and keep him or her informed about any changes.
- Avoid taking the same route every day at the same time.
- Select your own taxi cabs at random—don't take a cab that is not clearly identified as a taxi. Report any suspicious activity to local police and the nearest U.S. embassy or consulate.
- If possible, travel with others.
- Don't accept unexpected packages. Never carry a package or luggage for anyone else across a border.
- Always check your car for loose wires or other suspicious conditions before using it.

- Be sure your vehicle is in good operating condition with plenty of gas at all times. Drive with your windows closed when traveling on crowded streets. Bombs are sometimes thrown through open windows.
- If you are in a situation in which you hear explosions or gunfire, take cover or drop to the floor. Crawl to a safe area on your stomach, and don't move from your safe spot until you're sure the danger has passed.

CHAPTER 6

Playing It Safe: Reducing Recreational Risks

EVERY DAY, MILLIONS of Americans take to the great outdoors (and the great indoors, too) for recreation. While many of these endeavors are inherently dangerous—bungee jumping comes immediately to mind—most are only dangerous to participants if they don't know what they're doing or haven't had proper training.

This chapter is not intended as a substitute for specialized training or for studying the safety aspects of your favorite sport or recreation. Instead, its purpose is to give you an idea about some of the potential hazards before you decide to step into the water or go for a hike or a bike ride or participate in some other activity. It's also a good brushup for those of you who have had training but may be a little rusty. So take a few moments to review the safety suggestions in this chapter, then go ahead and enjoy your favorite sport . . . but be careful out there!

Boating

Ever take a boat out on a beautiful spring day? It seems that everyone else has the same idea. The Coast Guard estimates there are more than ten million registered boats in the United States. This figure doesn't include some boats like small sailboats or kayaks and canoes that don't need to be registered. Add these in and you're talking more than fifteen million recreational and commercial boats, and the number grows every year.

How many accidents occur? That's hard to say because the Coast Guard only hears about six thousand to seven thousand a year, but many experts say only about 10 percent of all accidents are reported, so the actual number could be as high as sixty to seventy thousand a year. As many as a thousand people a year may die due to boating accidents, including people who are employed on boats. Again, these numbers are only estimates. What's clear is that boating can be safe or dangerous depending upon how seriously you take the necessary precautions.

The most important safety factor is training. *Every boat owner should take a boating-safety course.* There are many places to get training such as from the Red Cross and the Coast Guard Auxiliary.

One of the cruel axioms about boating is, "If you have an emergency, you probably deserve it." This is not a pompous admonition by those who are wise about the ways of the waters against those who are new to the sport. Instead, it's a way of getting newcomers, and even old salts, to understand that *almost* every boating accident can be avoided. Not *all* of them are, of course, but the vast majority of boating accidents are preventable. Moreover, if an accident occurs, the proper training and equipment can help prevent fatalities.

The following safety measures aren't intended to be all-inclusive. The safety procedures you should obey depend upon what kind of boat you're operating, where you're operating it, how many people you have on board, and a host of other variables. Consider this section a starting point on your way to boat safety.

Before You Leave the Dock

Safe boating begins at the dock before you even cast off. All boaters should file a "float plan" that describes you, your crew and passengers, what kind of boat you have, its color and markings, where you are going, when you're coming back . . . you get the picture. This plan is designed to help rescuers find you if you're overdue. The Coast Guard and other groups have sample forms you can fill out and leave with a friend, neighbor, or relative on shore.

Check your boat for the mandatory safety equipment such as life jackets, and also make sure you have any additional equipment mandated by law. These optional items are also recommended:

- First aid kit and manual.
- Manual pump or bailer.
- Extra fuel, food, and water.
- Anchor and line.
- Radio for monitoring the weather.
- Marine transceiver for calling for help.
- Bullhorn
- Paddles or oars

Next, inspect your boat according to the instructions in the owner's manual. Make certain all fittings, lines, and engine components are in good condition. Check all your lights, charts, navigation equipment, fuel, and water supplies.

■ Overloading ■

One of the main causes of boating accidents, especially for small boats and canoes, is overloading. Don't assume that just because you can comfortably seat six people your vessel can safely carry that number. Overloading is the leading cause of swamping in rough weather (when water comes over the top edges into the boat) and swamping can lead to sinking. Overloading also makes the boat harder to steer and control, which can lead to capsizing (the boat turns upside down or on its side.)

Boats manufactured after November 1972 that are shorter than twenty feet long (except canoes, kayaks, inflatable rafts, and sailboats) are required to have labels giving the maximum capacity. Two figures are included: the total maximum capacity of the boat, which includes the weight of people, gear, and engine, and the maximum number of persons allowed to be on board. The number of persons is critical because it represents "live weight," the maximum number of people who can move around the boat safely without causing it to lose stability.

Even boats that aren't required to have capacity labels may have them anyway. However, if your boat does not carry such a label, you can calculate its capacity by multiplying the boat's length by its width and dividing by fifteen. This formula assumes each person weighs about 150 pounds.

Fueling is one of the most dangerous parts of boating. The danger comes from gas vapors, which are heavier than air, that collect in pockets of your boat. These vapor pockets are extremely volatile and can be ignited by a single spark, exploding with the force of dynamite. With safe practices, however, almost every fire or explosion can be prevented by following these safety tips for refueling:

- Turn off all electrical equipment before refueling, and don't turn any electrical equipment on.
- Don't smoke during fueling.
- Close doors and hatches to prevent gas fumes from entering the boat.
- Keep the fuel-hose nozzle in contact with the fuel tank filler pipe to prevent explosions caused by a static electricity spark.
- Wipe up any fuel spills immediately. Try to refuel in daylight or with plenty of flashlights playing on the area.
- When you're finished, open all doors and hatches to let any stray fumes escape. Smell around the boat for gas pockets.
- Let your boat sit for several minutes before you start the engines.

Show all passengers how to put on life jackets and let them see where they're located. Stow all gear securely so no one will be hit by loose items if the water gets rough. And before getting underway, know where you're going. Check your charts and plot a course.

Capsizing and falling overboard account for 60 percent of all boating fatalities. Statistic provided by the Coast Guard.

Knowledge is the most important part of boat safety. Know your boat, know the area, know the rules of boating, and know the weather.

Safety Musts

No matter what kind of boat you're on, federal law requires that you have certain safety devices. The Coast Guard, which administers and enforces the regulations, differentiates which devices you need based on the size of your vessel.

The most important safety device is the life jacket, also called a personal flotation device (PFD). If your vessel is less than sixteen feet long, you need one type of PFD or throwable flotation aid for each person. If your vessel is sixteen feet long or longer, you must have one PFD for each person plus at least one throwable flotation device. PFDs are rated as Type I, II, III, and V. Type IV is a throwable device like a life ring or cushion. (See the box adjoining this discussion for PFD type descriptions.)

Whenever dangerous water or weather conditions arise, put on your PFD immediately. Children and nonswimmers should always wear their PFDs, no matter what the conditions are like.

■ Flotation Devices ■

PFDs come in many sizes, styles, and colors. The type number is clearly marked on all PFDs. Each type is designed for a different use based on where you're going and what you're doing:

Type I. This is an offshore jacket designed for use in rough or remote waters where it may take some time for rescuers to reach you. It's designed to turn your face upward if you're rendered unconscious. Type I jackets are bulky and come in two sizes: children and adults.

Type II. This near-shore buoyant vest is suited to calm, inland waters where fast rescue is expected. It's less bulky than a Type I jacket but *will not always* turn unconscious wearers face-upward. It's not suited for rough seas. It comes in infant, small, and medium child and adult sizes.

Type III. This is generally the most comfortable jacket for continuous wear. *Flotation aids,* as they're called, are designed for calm, inland waters where there's a good chance for a quick rescue. You have more freedom of movement than the first two types so the type III device is suited for fishing, sailing, and other activities. It's not for rough water, though, and you'll have to tilt your head back to avoid getting water in your face when you're wearing it. Type III jackets come in many sizes from small child through adult.

Type IV. Throwable devices such as life rings and flotation cushions and "horseshoes" are for calm, inland waters where help is close by. They're designed for throwing to people who have slipped overboard. Obviously, they're not safe for nonswimmers, unconscious people, or for many hours in the water.

Type V. Special-use devices are only designed for use as listed on the label. Some special uses are boardsailing, work vests (worn by offshore oil-derrick workers, for example) and surfboarding. There is also a type V hybrid inflatable device that may be useful depending upon the application and conditions. These must be worn continuously to be counted as a regulation PFD. They are the least bulky of all types and comfortable to wear for long periods out of the water. However, once you are in the water, you must activate an air canister for it to inflate.

All PFDs should be checked before you get under way. Look for holes, cracks, rips, signs of mildew, and rusted hardware. Some PFDs can lose their buoyancy with age and use. All PFDs should be water tested at the beginning of each season. PFDs should fit snugly and keep your mouth above water. If yours doesn't, try a different one more suited to your weight and body type.

Make sure all passengers know where the PFDs are located. They should be easily accessible. The law doesn't require that adults wear their PFDs constantly while on the water. However, it's no surprise that the vast majority of people who drown are not wearing their PFDs. The best advice is to wear your PFD anytime you're out on the water. Most people don't wear PFDs because they're bulky and uncomfortable, so if you find one that fits well and is fairly comfortable, you're more likely to wear it. However, if anyone decides to take the risk and not wear a PFD, at least make certain he or she practices putting it on before leaving the dock. If an accident should occur, he or she will be ready.

■ Hypothermia ■

Your body cools down about twenty-five times faster in water than in air. Water less than seventy degrees Fahrenheit can rob your body of heat. If your body temperature goes too low, a condition known as hypothermia occurs, and you could pass out and drown.

The following chart shows how long most adults can expect to last in water before hypothermia sets in.

If the Water Temp. (F) is . . .	Exhaustion or Unconsciousness	Expected Time of Survival is . . .
32.5	Under 15 Min.	Under 15–45 Min.
32.5–40.0	15–30 Min.	30–90 Min.
40–50	30–60 Min.	1–3 Hr.
50–60	1–2 Hr.	1–6 Hr.
60–70	2–7 Hr.	2–40 Hr.
70–80	3–12 Hr.	3–Indefinitely
over 80	Indefinitely	

All powerboats must have a Coast Guard-approved fire extinguisher on-board except for outboard motorboats less than twenty-six feet long where the fuel vapors can't be trapped in any spaces.

All powerboats must have proper ventilation, and boats built after August 1980 must have installed blowers to clear flammable vapors. Carburetors on inboard gasoline engines must have backfire flame arresters.

You also must have on-board a whistle, bell, horn, or other noisemaker that can be heard for a half-mile. For boats longer than sixteen feet you must have distress-signal devices for day and night use such as red flares and distress lights and flags. For smaller boats, only nighttime signal devices are required.

Check with your local Coast Guard for the exact requirements for your boat. In addition, the Coast Guard has a toll-free boating-safety hot line (800-368-5647, or 267–0780 in Washington, D.C.) that you can call for up-to-date safety requirements and other boating safety information.

The boating-safety hot line can also be used to check recalls by boat manufacturers. If you're buying a used boat or engine, check with the hot line to find out if it's been recalled for safety reasons. If it has, the operator will send you information on how to get the manufacturer to correct the safety defect.

Marine Weather

Whether you're in a canoe or a sixty-five-foot yacht, weather plays a large part in boating safety. It's important to learn about the early warning signs of adverse weather and what to do when they occur.

Before leaving the dock, check the weather report. All areas in the country are within range of radio stations run by the National Oceanic and Atmospheric Administration (NOAA). These stations transmit regional weather on VHF radio and can be heard on scanner radios and also on special "weather radios" sold in electronics stores. When these stations are near waterways, they broadcast marine forecasts. If the report calls for storms, do not take your boat out.

If you don't have a weather radio, local cable TV systems may broadcast the "Weather Channel," which includes local conditions and forecasts, or you can also hear reports on local TV and radio stations. You can also ask a dockmaster or someone else at the marina about the weather forecast. Most people who work near boats keep an eye on the weather. It bears repeating: *Don't go out if the weather is threatening,* and when you do go out on the water keep an eye on the weather even if the forecast didn't mention the possibility of problems. Darkening skies, thunder, lightning, static on the radio, and cool blasts of wind are all indications of impending storms. Turn back immediately.

If you're caught in a storm, have everyone put on a life jacket. If you're in a sailing vessel, take down the sails and store them. If there is lightning, go as low in the boat as possible and as far from the masts as you can get. If your boat has a cabin, get inside.

If you can safely navigate, it's best to sail at right angles to waves, meeting them head-on instead of positioning your boat parallel to the wave action.

■ Capsizing ■

If your boat capsizes:

1. Have everyone put on a life jacket (ideally you've done this before the boat overturned, but if not help all passengers get into life jackets in the water).
2. Hang on to the boat; don't swim away. Stay together. It will enhance the chances of rescuers finding everyone. Even capsized boats float, especially newer ones, because they have extra flotation material inside the hull.
3. In cold water, conserve body heat by huddling together or putting your knees to your chest. If your PFD doesn't support your head, "stand" straight up in the water with your arms and legs together tightly.

Traffic Rules

Just like highways, waterways have rules of the road. No matter how big or small your boat is, you are required to follow these rules, which are not only part of customary boating etiquette but are also designed to prevent accidents.

- Powerboats must yield to sail boats. The reasoning is that powerboats have more control over their course while sailboats are at the mercy of the winds. While most powerboaters adhere to this rule, sailboaters should be alert at all times and not assume that they will be given the right of way.

- When two boats are heading straight toward each other, they should steer to the right.
- When crossing paths, the boat on the right has the right of way. The boat on the left should give way to the boat on the right. In marine terms, the boat on the right is "privileged," meaning it has the right of way. The boat on the left is "burdened," meaning it's required to change course or slow down to accommodate the "privileged" vessel.
- When one boat wants to pass another boat from the rear, it can do so on either side. However, the boat being passed is considered "privileged" and the passing boat must make sure not to get in its way or disturb its course.

Whenever possible, use a marine radio to contact other boats about your intentions (passing, for instance) on channel 16, the calling and distress channel, to help avoid accidents.

Alcohol

Of the people who die from boating accidents, nine out of ten drown and 50 percent of these drownings are related to alcohol, the Coast Guard says. Quite simply, alcohol is the single most important factor in boating deaths.

Public awareness, increased law enforcement efforts, and pressure from citizens groups have helped to stem the use of alcohol by automobile drivers, but boating under the influence of drugs or alcohol has not received the same attention. The problem is clearly cultural; the concept of boating has always been about having fun and being free and unencumbered. For many people, this means drinking alcohol.

Unfortunately, alcohol becomes a much more potent drug on the water than it would on land. *Boater's hypnosis* is a condition brought about by several hours of hot sun spent riding on a rolling boat surrounded by vibration, wind, and noise. Under these conditions your reactions become slower, as if you were drunk. And you're usually tired too. Combined with this factor, drinking only a few beers impairs your ability to reason as well as your reaction time. If an emergency arises, if you were to fall overboard, for example, you would be less equipped to handle it. Drinking and boating don't mix.

Canoes

Canoes are wonderful vessels, but they get a bad wrap in TV sitcoms, where people are always standing up, waving their arms wildly, and going over the side.

While it's funny on TV, falling out of a canoe isn't much fun in real life, and it can be dangerous. Follow these tips for safe canoeing:

- Keep your center of gravity low at all times, especially when moving from one part of the canoe to another.
- Board the canoe at your paddling position whenever possible. This will eliminate your having to move around the canoe.
- Step from the shore to the bottom center of the canoe.
- Kneeling on the bottom of the canoe will give you maximum stability and control.
- If the canoe should capsize, don't panic. If you end up under the canoe, hold on to it with your hands and stay upside down long enough to get your feet and legs free of the canoe, if necessary. Then surface (watching out so you don't bump your head on the canoe!) and swim back toward the canoe. Hold on to the canoe until help arrives.

Swimming

Let's stay in the water and talk about swimming, the most popular outside recreation in the United States. Its popularity cuts across all age groups. Unfortunately, about three thousand people drowned outside the home in 1991, and most of these were children under the age of four. In fact, drowning is the second leading cause of non-motor-vehicle deaths outside the home for all age groups, and this doesn't include drownings due to boating accidents.

Many of these accidental deaths could have been averted with proper water-safety training. More than any other precaution, learning how to swim or stay afloat is the most important factor in preventing accidental drowning. Everyone should learn what's known as *drown-proofing* or *survival floating*. Even people who don't know how to swim can learn to stay afloat for a long time without expending a lot of energy by using this method. In fact, survival floating is extremely efficient because it conserves body energy, a crucial part of escaping hypothermia while in cold water.

Survival floating makes use of the body's natural buoyancy. There are five steps:

1. **The resting position:** The body is limp, relaxed. Take a deep breath and sink vertically. Your arms should hang down by your sides. Your mouth is under water.
2. **Preparing to surface:** Slowly lift your arms in front of your head, raising one knee toward your chest and extend the other leg behind your body as if you were going to run in slow motion.
3. **Exhale:** Raise your head up with your mouth just out of the water and exhale.
4. **Inhale:** Kick gently and sweep your arms slowly to raise your body up just high enough so your chin is above the surface. Breathe in.
5. **Return to the resting position:** As you sink down, resume the same position as in step 1, above. Drop your chin to your chest and relax your body.

All these motions should be slow. The idea is to conserve energy until you're rescued. Everyone should practice this technique. Even if you're an accomplished swimmer, you should learn how to do it. There may be instances when you are too tired to swim or land is too far away to reach or you're too injured to swim.

General Rules for All Swimmers

You've heard this rule since you were a child. It's always "Rule Number One": **Never swim alone.** Either swim with a buddy or make sure someone is watching you swim.

Never swim when you're tired or cold.

At the beach, watch out for undertow and rip currents in the ocean. These swift-moving currents can take you far away from where you want to be. The best precaution is to know the area and heed the lifeguard's warnings about areas with tricky currents. If you're caught in a current, don't fight it. Go with it, swimming parallel to the current until you're free, then head for shore.

When swimming in rivers and streams, watch out for slick rocks and holes on the bottom. Keep away from swift-running currents and avoid white-water areas. White water is caused by swift-moving water saturated with air bubbles usually as the result of waterfalls or rapids. It's tough to swim in white water because the air makes it less buoyant. White water can also hide dangerous rocks and it can have hydraulics, tornado-like whirlpools that can drag you deeper into the water. If you're stuck in a hydraulic, don't fight. Hold your breath and try to protect your head from buffeting against rocks. Eventually, hydraulics will deposit you downstream, although some people have gotten caught in them and needed assistance to break free. Some very strong swimmers are able to swim under the hydraulic, if there's space, and swim away. The best advice is keep away from rapids.

Pools

Pools present a different set of hazards. All pools should have locked fences around them to prevent unauthorized entry. Fences should be four to six feet high to prevent children from entering the area, because stories about children wandering into pools and drowning are all too common. In some jurisdictions, fences around pools are a zoning requirement.

Pools also are notorious areas for accidental falls. The situation is perfect: no shoes, wet walkways, and slippery surfaces. Always wear shoes near pools unless you're going for a swim. Nobody expects you to walk around with a mop, but make sure guests are aware of wet, slippery areas.

Never swim under or around the diving board.

All pools should have depth markers so visitors can be wary of shallow areas. In fact, the host should make it a point to tell visitors about the depth of the pool. Most pools vary in depth from one end to the other.

Diving

One of the biggest dangers in pools is diving. Each year, more than 800 people suffer spinal injuries from diving-related accidents. Another 100,000 sustain injuries severe enough to require medical attention. The victim is usually a man between eighteen and thirty who has never dived before. Alcohol is often a factor.

Most diving accidents are the same. The diver, who has never had diving instructions, dives into water that is too shallow, and hits his or her head with great force on the bottom. In the past several years, diving boards have been taken out of many hotel and public pools to discourage diving, and many pools have erected signs warning that diving from the edge of the pool is also prohibited. Diving is indeed dangerous, and the best advice for most people is not to dive. In fact, water-safety programs aimed at children and teenagers discourage casual diving and emphasize "feet-first" jumping.

SAFETY BY THE NUMBERS

In 1990, 107 people succumbed to recreational diving fatalities.

Certified life-saving programs also encourage feet-first rescues for two reasons. First, the rescuer should never take his or her eyes off the person being rescued and second, a dive could result in the rescuer's hitting bottom and getting knocked out.

If you want to dive, do so only under close supervision and with proper instruction. You will also learn to steer up as soon as you hit the water. Even in deep water, there is a chance of hitting bottom. Diving can be a beautiful sport, but it is dangerous unless closely supervised.

Jaws? Not really.

Despite what you see in the movies, being attacked by a shark is a rather rare occurrence, especially in the United States. Generally, lifeguards and others familiar with a particular beach know if there are sharks around. These people are your best source of information about whether it's safe to swim.

While shark attacks are rare, other sea creatures pose a more common threat to your health. Jellyfish, for example, inhabit oceans and some bays and sounds, and their sting can hurt. For most of us, a jellyfish sting is on the same level as a bee sting: not fatal, but it can cause great discomfort and swelling. If you're stung by a jellyfish, wash the wound thoroughly (with saltwater if possible) and dab on alcohol of some kind (use alcohol-containing substances such as liquor or perfume, etc., if that's all you have) or use ammonia, which nullifies the venom. Powdered meat tenderizer containing *papain* also helps to counteract the venom. If the tentacles are clinging to your skin, remove them promptly, but don't touch them with your bare hand.

It's important to keep an eye on the wound. If it swells or becomes infected, get medical attention.

If you know you're allergic to insect bites, bee stings, and similar annoyances you should seek medical attention immediately. There's a good chance you will be allergic to jellyfish stings also.

The best advice for keeping out of trouble is not to swim in areas that have jellyfish. Again, the local lifeguard or others familiar with the area can tell you if they've seen jellyfish.

When swimming you should also ask if there are any urchins or fire coral in the area. These can also sting if you step on them. Wear sneakers or diving booties or keep away.

Stingrays are fan-shaped fish that often hide in the sand close to shore, and it's difficult to see them. They look scarier than they really are. In fact, stingrays are scared of people and will swim away if confronted. They never attack humans, but it's common for people to step on them and sometimes get the stingray's stinger embedded in their feet. Unlike a jellyfish, stingray venom is more dangerous. The area will usually swell and turn black and blue. You may feel nauseous, dizzy, and weak after being stung.

Fortunately, keeping out of stingray trouble is fairly easy. Wearing sneakers or booties helps, but you should also shuffle your feet along the floor of the ocean to scare the stingrays away. If the water is clear, keep an eye out for them.

Fishing

Before we leave the water, let's look at fishing, which seems like a happy and safe sport—and it usually is. After all, how much trouble can you get into sitting in a serene spot waiting for the fish to bite?

Actually, there are some hazards you should be aware of before you set out. Besides falling out of a boat, which we already discussed in the boating section of this chapter, falling off of rocks while fishing is a common occurrence that contains a double whammy. If the fall doesn't kill you, drowning in the water could! Never wade in a stream by yourself. Sudden drops, holes, and unseen debris occur in all bodies of water. Wear waders that give you maximum foot traction and walk very slowly. Test each step before committing your weight to it.

Rocks can be extremely slippery, especially when they're smoothed by running water and covered with algae or other plants. Use extra caution in areas where you can't see the bottom.

The most common fishing injury is from hooks. Treble hooks are great for catching fish but nasty when they catch people. When you're casting, keep away from other people. And if you're lucky enough to catch a fish, reel it in slowly. Not only is it safer and less harmful for the fish, but it's also safer and less harmful for you if the hook should slip out of the fish and slingshot back at you.

If you get stuck with a hook, seek medical attention—if you can. Most often, fishing is far away from medical facilities, so you'll have to take care of yourself. If the barb is not exposed, it may be best to continue pushing the hook

■ Here Comes the Sun ■

A deep suntan has often been the sign of the leisure class, indicating that a person actually had time to work on getting the perfect tan. Now the word is out about the sun: tans may make you look healthy (this in itself is a cultural bias,) but there's nothing healthy about the effects of the sun—wrinkles, dry skin, and skin cancer.

If you're going to enjoy the outdoors, pay attention to the sun. Even short exposure times can burn you before you realize it. Always use sunscreen or sunblock. Sunblock blocks and reflects ultraviolet rays. Sunscreen absorbs the rays. Go for the sunblock, especially if it's very hot outside.

The lighter your skin, the higher the Sun Protection Factor, or SPF, you should use. SPF numbers range from two to forty-five; the higher the number the greater the protection. Even dark-skinned people are not immune from the harmful effects of the sun. They should use some protection as well.

Avoid being in the sun during the peak hours of 10 A.M. to 3 P.M., and remember that just because it's cloudy, it doesn't mean that the ultraviolet rays aren't reaching you. Wear a hat and sunglasses if possible. If you're counting on a T-shirt or sweater for sun protection, be aware that the closer the weave, the more protection you'll enjoy.

Be very careful when you're on the water, where you're not only being exposed to direct rays but reflected rays.

If you enjoy snow skiing or snow hiking, be especially cognizant of the sun's rays at high altitudes. They can be more powerful there than at sea level because there's less atmosphere to filter the sunlight. In addition, you're getting reflected sunlight off the snow. Always wear sunglasses in the snow. Bright sunlight can temporarily impair your eyes, making them less sensitive to light. This is called *snow blindness,* and it's usually not a problem until the evening when you're trying to see in the dark. If you have a severe case, it could take several hours to get your *night vision* back.

through the skin until it comes out. Of course, you won't do this if the natural path of the hook goes through bone or is deep in the flesh or a sensitive area such as your eye. If you're fortunate enough to be able to push the barb out, cut it off with a wire cutters. This will allow you to get the de-barbed hook out at the point of entry without further damaging your skin. Wash the wound with antiseptic, bandage it, and get a tetanus shot as soon as possible.

Learn how to hold different kinds of fish while removing the hook. Some fish have sharp, protruding spines and fins that can cut hands. And some fish bite. Grasp the fish securely and use a pair of pliers (or a hook remover) to help retrieve the hook.

Other Warm-Weather Sports

Now that we're finally out of the water, let's discuss some hazards involved in some other popular warm-weather sports.

Hiking and Camping

Hiking is usually not a dangerous endeavor. With the proper training and equipment, you should have a safe outing when you go hiking.

The most important factor for comfortable and safe hiking is shoes. For long hikes, plain old (or even fancy new) sneakers won't cut it. You should wear hiking shoes or boots if you're going to be trekking any great distance. Besides making your feet miserable, inappropriate or ill-fitting footwear can cause blisters and chafing. In the worst case, it can also cause you to lose your footing on rocks, and that can be especially dangerous. If you're in the wilderness, any injuries, including twisted ankles, plunge you into trouble.

When choosing the correct fit, your best guide is a knowledgeable salesperson. He or she will be able to help you get the best footwear for the size and shape of your foot. The salesperson will also instruct you about the socks you should wear with the hiking boots. You should try on new boots with the same kind of socks you'll be wearing on your hikes. Bring them from home (or purchase them there—most stores that sell hiking boots also sell appropriate socks to wear with them). Many people like to wear two pairs of socks when they're hiking: a lightweight pair of cotton socks next to their skin to help absorb sweat, and a heavier wool or cotton outer sock to keep the feet warm and help absorb shocks.

■ If You Get Lost ■

Rule Number One: Don't Panic.

Yes, that's easy to say now, but it's more than just a suggestion to make you feel better if you're lost. It's the beginning of a tried-and-true method for getting out of your predicament.

If you get lost, stay calm, and don't run around looking for where you went wrong. Sit down and study the situation rationally. Check your maps and your compass. Are you really lost, or did you just make a wrong turn a few miles back?

When you think about it, you'll probably find that you have an idea where you are based on the direction you were heading, how long you've been traveling, nearby landmarks, and so forth. For example, if you're near a stream and it's the only stream around, then you're not too lost. You can always follow the stream downhill to civilization.

Don't guess where you are and then head somewhere based on a another guess. Formulate a plan based on what you know from your map and compass, and then pursue that plan. If you know a road is north of where you are, head for it. If you know the river flows to a town, follow it. In other words, don't try to be clever in finding a complicated way back to your campsite. Go for the sure thing. Here are some more tips for safe hiking:

- Trails going down mountains usually lead to towns.
- Most streams flow to civilization.
- Head for power or phone lines. They will lead to civilization.
- If you see lights at night, head in that direction in the morning.
- Railroad tracks will eventually lead to civilization.

If all else fails, if you've lost your compass and map and haven't got a clue where you are, sit tight. Someone will come looking for you. (You did leave word with someone where you'd be hiking, didn't you?) It's better to dig in and remain safe than to ramble around aimlessly. If the weather is cold, build a shelter and stay put.

You can help rescuers by building smoky fires or finding a field and writing SOS with stones or pieces of wood. If you have a gun, use it to signal rescuers. Three times in rapid succession is a standard "find-me-I'm-lost" message.

Once you buy your hiking boots, you should break them in by wearing them around the house and during short walks around the neighborhood. This will not only give you a chance to get used to walking in these boots—they will probably be heavier than anything you've ever worn except for snow boots—but it will also let you know if they're not fitting correctly so you can adjust or return them.

Some people say the neophyte hiker will inevitably suffer blisters, but that's an old notion that shouldn't be true anymore. Modern hiking shoes have come a long way in design, and blisters are not the *fait accompli* they once were. However, always be alert to the possibility of blisters before they happen. Always carry *moleskin,* a flat material with adhesive on one side and padding on the other, when you hike. Place the moleskin on the problem area before you actually raise a blister, and you may not get one.

Experienced hikers also carry an extra pair of shoes, like moccasins or sneakers, for the campsite. It's good for your shoes to let them air out and dry at the end of a day's hike. It's also a good idea sometimes to switch to your extra pair of shoes when you're crossing a stream. This will keep your hiking boots dry for the rest of the trip.

Here are other suggestions to keep your trip safe:

- Don't start a hike in threatening weather. This is especially true for mountain climbers. The weather at the top isn't going to be better than the weather at the bottom. Usually it's worse.
- **Always let someone know where you're going and how long you will be away.**
- Don't walk beyond your limits. Remember, you have to walk back out again.
- Factor in high altitude and its debilitating effects. If you haven't trained for high-altitude hiking, don't do it.
- Don't feed wild animals. Bears can be especially dangerous, even if they're used to people.
- Be careful crossing railroad tracks. Look both ways and never step on switching tracks. You could get your foot caught.

- Be careful when you're stepping on smooth rocks. They can be more slippery then you think.
- Never reach your hand into rock crevices or hollow trees unless you can see inside. Snakes may live there!
- Rest if you're tired. Most accidents and falls occur when you're fatigued.
- Don't drink from streams unless you know personally about the water's purity. If you must drink water from springs or streams take the proper steps to purify it.
- Don't eat any fruit, berry, or mushroom in the wild unless you're certain you know what it is.

There's one more rule that you and many other people will break regularly—but shouldn't. **Never hike alone.** You're always well advised to travel with other people because in the wilderness, even a small accident can become life threatening. With that said, it's also a fact of life that many of us desire the peace and serenity that comes from hiking by ourselves. It's a chance to get in touch with our inner beings, to experience our own private thoughts and to nurture self-confidence.

So, while it's advisable to hike with someone else, it's understandable that solo hiking is so rewarding you might want to accept the risk. It's your choice; but at the very least, make sure you're well equipped and well prepared if you're going into the wilderness. And make sure you let someone know where you're going and when you'll be back.

Are you done walking? Going to rest for the night? Then you're probably . . .

Camping

Sleeping outside under the stars is one of the great pleasures of life. It's quiet, serene, and for those of us who live in the city, it's wonderfully dark with no artificial street lights to encroach on the evening.

Camping, like hiking, is an inherently safe sport, but this doesn't mean you can just go out and camp. You need the right equipment and a general know-how about the woods.

One of the few dangers in camping is fires. Many forest fires are caused by careless campers who are soon trapped by the blaze they've started. Animals and trees are also the victims of accidental forest fires. Before you roast that first marshmallow of the evening think about fire safety. And after that last cup of coffee is brewed and you're about to get cozy in your sleeping bag, think about fire safety again.

The best advice is not to build fires at all. Many campers use carry-in stoves that use propane or other fuels. They're lightweight, efficient, and they save trees. However, if you need a fire for cooking or warmth—and it's allowed in the area where you're camping—follow these rules:

- Never build a fire on pine needles or other forest debris. They can smolder, then ignite after you've left the campground. Instead, clear all branches and leaves for several feet around your campfire so shooting sparks can't ignite them.
- Never build a fire under low-hanging branches.
- Never leave a blazing fire unattended.
- Never build a fire in an area that's under a fire emergency. All federal, state, and county parks use a scale where they rate the fire hazard due to drought or low rainfall. Check with the park ranger or look for the fire danger signs at the park entrance and heed the warning.
- If possible don't burn soft, resinous, sappy woods like pine that give off lots of sparks. Only burn dead wood.
- **Make sure your fire is out when you leave the campsite.** Check it thoroughly. Pour water on the ashes if you can. If not, bury the ashes in dirt, then stir the ashes again and examine them to make sure there are no burning embers. Don't leave the area if you see any smoke or if there's any heat still coming from the fire area.

Sleeping in tents presents some hazards that you should know about. There is always the danger that campers will die from carbon monoxide poisoning because they've placed heaters or stoves inside and filled the tent with carbon monoxide.

Obviously, this problem occurs most often during cold weather. Snow campers are particularly at risk because the doors are usually closed, and snow may cover any possible ventilation slits or holes. Carbon monoxide poisoning gives little warning; it is an odorless and colorless gas.

Take precautions when you're cooking in a tent or using a heater. Make sure the windows are open or that you're getting ventilation through the door. (Tents rated for cooking have ventilation/cooking holes, and they're the only safe way to go.) If snow is falling, keep checking that the ventilation holes aren't being covered. Drifts can build quickly.

Even if you're not cooking inside your tent, be wary of falling snow, which can cover ventilation holes and prevent the tent from "breathing." This allows a buildup of the carbon dioxide you exhale and may cause asphyxiation—too much carbon dioxide and too little oxygen. If you're sleeping, your body will wake you up, gasping for air. It's an involuntary response. The danger is that even though you wake up, you may be too weak to open the tent and get the ventilation you need to survive. In addition, if it's extremely cold outside, you might expose yourself to the elements just to breathe some fresh air—then suffer from the effects of the low temperatures and wind.

Remember, too, that tents are not designed to withstand a lot of snow on the roofs. If the snowfall is particularly heavy and wet, you might consider leaving your warm sleeping bag every once in a while to brush the snow off the roof. If you don't, it could collapse.

Bears

While it's amusing to see cartoon creatures like Yogi Bear steal picnic baskets right from under campers' noses, it's not so funny in real life. In many heavily used campground areas, like those in national parks, bears have lost their fear of people. Rangers worry about this because bears that are unafraid of people are no less dangerous. In fact, they can become more dangerous to humans because they're willing to come closer to them in established camping areas.

Bears come into the campgrounds for one reason—to eat food that people leave around. They have become used to this source of food and continue to look for it, sometimes getting mean about. Rangers try to break the bears of this habit of relying on people for food by cautioning campers never to feed the bears. Unfortunately, some campers don't heed this advice. They still think it's cute to feed the animals.

Even if you don't intentionally feed the bears, it's important that you don't store food in your tent because bears have been known to slash open tents if they smell a potential meal. Instead, hang food from a tree—upwind from your campsite—and burn all food wastes so you don't attract bears to your area. Don't spill any juices or oils on the ground around the campsite.

When you're traveling in bear country keep in mind that bears don't look for people to eat, but they will attack if confronted or challenged. There's no one right way to act every time if you meet a bear, but here are some tactics that may work. It may sound odd, but whether these ideas do the trick depends upon how often the bear has been exposed to people.

- Stand your ground and back away slowly if the bear is close to you. If you've got your pack on your back, loosen and drop it. The bear would much rather eat your food than you. Talking slowly and softly sometimes helps. Very often the bear will check you out and leave.
- If you've got something that makes a loud noise (like firecrackers or a gun,) use it. Even yelling might work. In the "old days" in national parks, bears could be chased away by the noise of people hitting pots and pans together. The bears seem to ignore it these days; they're used to it.
- If everything else fails, head for the nearest tree, and it better be close because bears are fast. You may be safe as long as you're looking down at the bear's head.
- As a last resort, people have saved themselves by turn-

ing into a fetal position and protecting their face with their hands. The bear may paw you around then become bored and leave.

Snakes

The good news is that while snakebites can be lethal, they're relatively rare. Snakes usually won't attack people unless they're bothered. Even then, they'd much rather flee than fight. If you encounter a snake, don't corner it. Give it a chance to get away, and most of the time it will leave you alone.

Only a minority of the overall number of snakes, about 20 out of 125 species in the United State, are poisonous. As cities and towns encroach upon outlying areas, destroying snakes' habitat, the actual number of all snakes is dropping rapidly. In this country, there are only two distinct kinds of poisonous snakes: coral snakes and pit vipers.

Coral snakes are usually under three feet long; they are slender with smooth, shiny scales. Their head is about the same diameter as the body; there is no transition area between head and body. The nose is black and the body is covered with rings of red, black, and yellow. Coral snakes are poisonous, but cases of their biting humans are rare. They're found in the southwestern United States.

Pit vipers include rattlesnakes, cottonmouths or water moccasins, and copperheads. Pit vipers are so named because of a pit between each eye and a nostril. The fangs are paired.

More than twenty-five kinds of rattlesnakes exist in the United States, and they all share the distinctive rattle or button on the end of their tail. Unlike rattlesnakes in cartoons, real rattlesnakes don't make a loud rattle. It's generally quieter and much lower in tone than you may have been led to believe. They rattle their tails when they're disturbed. Rattlesnakes come in different colors and in all sizes, from a foot or two to more than eight feet long.

Copperheads are correctly named. Their heads are copper colored. Between two and three feet long, copperheads have venom in their fangs but its effects are rarely fatal. The body is light brown or light reddish brown with chestnut-brown colored Y-shaped marks on the sides.

Cottonmouths, or water moccasins, live near lakes, ponds, and streams. They're dull brown, sometimes an olive green, and they grow to about three feet although some are larger. The name cottonmouth comes about because when the snake opens its mouth, which it does as a scare tactic, the inside of the mouth is white.

If you're going to be traveling in snake country, you should carry a snakebite kit, wear high boots and keep your eyes open. For the most part, snakes don't like heat or direct sun and will hide under rocks or burrow into the dirt during the day. If you're traveling at night, be sure to use a flashlight.

As we discussed earlier, **never put your hands in rock crevices without checking them first for snakes.** And never sit on cool rocks to rest until you've checked the area for snake hiding places.

Insects

In the United States more people die from the bites of insects—hornets, bees, wasps, and spiders—than from snakebites. Fortunately, most of us won't have a severe reaction to an insect bite, also called *anaphylaxis*. But if you are allergic, you should carry an emergency bug-bite kit when you venture outdoors. These kits usually contain some form of atropine in a syringe, which you give yourself once you've been bitten, and they may also have antihistamines, a tourniquet, a magnifying glass, and tweezers to remove the stinger.

How do you know if you have an allergy to bee stings if you've never been stung? You don't, but your doctor can tell you if you are predisposed to react to insect bites based on your medical history. Sometimes, but not always, people with asthma and other allergies may also be sensitive to insect bites. If you've had one bad reaction to an insect bite, the second time may be more severe.

If you're stung by an insect that leaves a stinger, it's important to remove that stinger immediately. Sucking the venom out will also help. If you have any reaction such as dizziness, difficultly breathing, or nausea you should seek medical attention.

There are measures you can take to keep the pesky critters from finding you attractive. First, don't wear light-colored clothing; bugs like light colors. Also, don't wear perfumes, after-shaves, or any sort of scented lotions. Use one of the many excellent bug repellents now on the market.

Bugs are often attracted by sweet fruits, so be sure to wipe your face and hands after you've eaten that juicy orange.

Ticks

One insect all of us should be especially wary of is the tick. It's important to keep your legs and feet covered when traveling in dense forests where ticks are known to exist. Many people tuck their pants legs into their socks or boots. Wear a hat and use insect repellent.

It usually takes a few hours for ticks to get attached to your skin, so check yourself all over a couple of times a day or at least in the evening if you've been in heavy "tick country." Pay special attention to your hair and ears.

Ticks burrow into your skin and anchor there. If you try to pull them out, you may break the insect in two, leaving the head still attached. One way to remove ticks is to touch it with a hot match head (being careful not to burn yourself). The tick will often remove itself when it feels the heat. Another method is to soak the tick with alcohol. This will usually kill the tick and you can pull it out. Mineral oil also works well because it suffocates the tick, causing it to withdraw. Still another method is to grasp the tick with a tweezers and slowly pull it out. This is a good method if the tick hasn't burrowed itself too deeply. Always make sure you get all the pieces of the tick out of your skin.

Ticks can transmit several dangerous diseases. One is *Rocky Mountain spotted fever*. The symptoms of this disease come on slowly and are characterized by a rash about three or four days after contact. You may also feel chills, headaches, and fever. Antibiotics have been found to be successful in treating this malady.

A more dangerous problem is *Lyme disease,* named after Lyme, Connecticut, where it was first isolated and studied. Caused by a deer tick, Lyme disease has few early symptoms, and often sufferers don't know there's a problem until it's too late. The ticks that carry Lyme disease mostly infest deer, mice, and some other animals, and are now found throughout many areas of the country. It's even been found in other countries. Unlike other ticks, which are usually the size and shape of a small coffee bean, deer ticks are very small— so small, in fact, that you don't always notice them.

Within a month after being bitten by a tick carrying the disease a rash may appear. It doesn't hurt and it may disappear, so people often dismiss it. Other symptoms may include severe headaches, fever, lethargy, and chills. Within a few months, the heart muscle can become inflamed and the victim may suffer severe pain and meningitis. Within two years, the infected person may have arthritis-like symptoms that can become chronic.

The key to preventing tick-carried diseases is to keep away from tick-infested areas. If that's not possible, wear clothing that covers your skin, especially around the ankles. A few days or weeks after you've been in the woods, if you see a rash develop, even one that doesn't hurt or spread, see your doctor immediately. Early treatment with antibiotics can stem this deadly disease.

Plants

"Leaves of three, let it be."

This is not only a rhyme, it's good advice that's been handed down for generations. The most common toxic "leaves-of-three" plant is *poison ivy.* For most of us it's more of an annoyance than an outright danger, but for people who are allergic to its poison, the plant can present a health risk. Even for those who are only mildly allergic, as many of us are, the poison can become dangerous if it spreads to sensitive areas such as our mouths, ears, and around the eyes and genitals.

The poison is spread by rubbing against the plant and getting it on your skin. It can also be spread by dogs and cats that can carry the resin on their coats (although they won't be affected themselves). Poison ivy's resin can also be spread by touching clothing, especially shoes, that have come in contact with the plant.

The best way to prevent this problem is not to touch the plant. Everyone should learn to recognize poison ivy and related plants such as *poison oak* and *poison sumac.*

You can "catch" poison ivy year-round. In summer, the leaves are shiny, dark green, and in the fall they turn bright orange or red. In its fastest-growing period during spring and early summer, the plant shows white leaves, which develop into tiny green berries that then turn white in the fall.

The distinguishing features are the three-leaf clusters on short stalks that are different lengths. The leaves themselves may be smooth or serrated. The plant itself is usually a small bush, but sometimes it climbs like a nonpoisonous ivy. Poison ivy can be found almost everywhere.

Poison oak got its name from its leaves, which look like small oak leaves and are also clustered in groups of three. It's usually a small shrub, but sometimes it's a vine that clings or climbs up trees and other bushes. The berries are similar to those on poison ivy plants.

Poison sumac is less common than poison oak or poison ivy because it's mainly found in marshy areas. It's a bush but also can be found as a twenty- to twenty-five-foot tree resembling an ash. The leaves are sharply pointed and are arranged in pairs, with seven to thirteen pairs in a cluster and a single leaf at the end. The berries are cream-colored and grow in clusters along the side of the branches.

If you must go in areas with poison ivy, poison oak, or poison sumac, make sure your skin is covered by heavy clothing, including gloves. **Don't touch your gloves to your face at any time.**

If you think your clothes are heavily laced with the oily resin, wash them separately from other clothes in very hot water and detergent. You may want to wash them twice and then turn the washing machine on without any clothes inside just to make sure the resin is gone from the machine. You might also consider having your clothes dry cleaned. (Wrap the clothes in plastic and let the cleaner know there's poison ivy involved.)

The best way to rid poison ivy from your property is to kill the plants with special herbicides. Some people have also physically removed the plants, but that's a tough job and should only be undertaken by someone who doesn't have the slightest sensitivity to the poison. Even then, he or she should wear protective clothing. In the past, these plants were burned, but that's been found to be dangerous as the smoke carries the resin aloft. There have been cases of the poison getting in people's throats and lungs. It's best to let the plant dry then dispose of it in a landfill or other area, but be careful of the dead plants; they can still carry the resin.

Hunting

Hunting is an inherently dangerous sport because it involves the use of deadly weapons. Most hunting accidents are the result of carelessness and ignorance not because of malfunctioning firearms or some other factor beyond our control. In addition, not all accidents involving hunting weapons happen during hunting activities or even during hunting season. Many fatalities occur in and around the home, with the majority of gun fatalities happening to people under the age of twenty-one.

Make sure everyone in your family who owns or handles firearms follows these safety tips.

SAFETY BY THE NUMBERS

In 1990, there were about 137 fatal and 1,376 nonfatal hunting accidents in the United States, excluding Alaska. About 30 percent of the deaths and injuries were self-inflicted.

- Treat every gun as if it were loaded.
- Always hold the firearm so that the muzzle points

away from you and everyone else you're near. Then if it goes off, no one will be hit.

- Always keep your finger off the trigger until you're ready to shoot.
- Be sure you clearly identify your target and know what is beyond it.
- Keep the firearm unloaded until you're ready to use it.
- Make sure the barrel is unobstructed and that the firearm is in good working order.
- Use the proper ammunition.
- Avoid climbing over fences or negotiating other difficult terrain while carrying a firearm.
- Never drink alcohol while using a firearm.
- Store firearms and ammunition separately. Both should be inaccessible to children and other unauthorized people.
- Learn as much as you can about your firearm. Take safety classes.
- While hunting in the woods, make yourself visible to other hunters by wearing fluorescent colors. "Hunter orange" is very effective at dusk, and in many states it's required during certain hunting seasons.
- Teach children that firearms are not toys.

Caving

Caving is a wonderful, educational, and fascinating sport that's becoming very popular. There is ample opportunity to enjoy this activity because there are more than twenty thousand known caves in the United States alone, and some states, like Kentucky, Tennessee, and Alabama have thousands of caves each.

Caving is not only an opportunity to visit a world far removed from our everyday surroundings but also a chance to study nature in a unique environment. Also called *spelunking,* caving is a relatively safe sport because most people explore caves in groups with experienced cavers. These experienced leaders make a lot of preparations before entering a cave, and much of their work is aimed at keeping the adventure safe.

According to the National Speleological Society, falls account for the bulk of caving accidents, about 70 percent. Drownings come second, being hit by falling rocks is third, and failure of rappelling and climbing equipment is fourth.

Inexperience was cited as the overwhelming cause of these accidents, followed by inadequate equipment and poor judgment. Other causes included getting lost, getting stuck, losing your light, exposure, and flooding.

If you think you'd like to be a caver, a good place to start is a commercially operated cave, a place where you pay your money and are taken on a tour. This is a good and safe way to discover if you are interested in caves. It also gives you a safe way to learn if you're claustrophobic (afraid of confined spaces) or afraid of the dark. Because caves often have high ledges, it will also give you the opportunity to test your willingness to be at great heights.

If this trip whets your appetite for caves, the next step is to contact a local caving group. You can usually find them through your sporting outfitter, who may refer you to the local "grotto" of the National Speleological Society. These groups often have trips geared toward novices. It's a good way to explore noncommercial caves safely on your first time out.

Because the right equipment is crucial for enjoyable and safe spelunking, you should try to rent what you need instead of buying it. Don't invest in gear until you're sure you really like this stuff.

Although caving is usually a safe activity, like any other sport it carries the potential for danger. The number-one rule is the same as the most important rule in so many other sports: **never go caving alone.** The minimum number of people necessary, according to most cavers, is three, but the optimum minimum is four, including at least two who are experienced cavers.

Follow these additional tips to help keep your caving experiences accident-free.

- If you're new to caving, travel with experienced people.
- Keep your equipment in tip-top shape, and recheck it before you enter the cave.
- Carry at least three sources of spare lights and parts. Have enough power for twice your estimated trip.
- Always tell someone outside where you're going and when you expect to return.
- Wear the proper clothing. Pay special attention to wearing the right shoes, hardhats, and gloves.
- Stay together. Don't wander away from the group.
- Mark your route with ecologically friendly tape or some other item so you can find your way out.
- Learn as much about the cave as you can before entering.
- *Never* explore old mines. They can be dangerous.
- *Never* go caving when you're ill or taking medications that could alter your judgment or impair you in any way.
- Don't push yourself beyond your limits as you venture into the cave. Remember, you have to travel back out too.
- Don't use ladders or ropes that have been left behind by others unless you know that they are safe to use.
- Never light a fire inside a cave. Fires consume oxygen, and in addition, bat guano is flammable. Whole sections of caves could burn if they are covered by these droppings.
- Be wary of caves with streams and rivers. They could overflow and flood during a storm. Check the weather before you explore.

Because a cave will look different going out than going in, it's crucial that you turn around every once in a while to see what the way out looks like.

Leave ecologically sound markings in areas such as junctions and large rooms that may be tricky on your return. Remove the markings as you leave. In the early days of caving, many cavers marked trails with paint or soot from their lamps. This is not done anymore by responsible cavers. Don't heed these older markings; you can't be sure what the previous caver was indicating. The arrow may point to the way out—or it might lead you in the opposite direction, toward some interesting structure.

If you should get lost in a cave, sit down and consider what you remember about the trail. Among your group, there may be a correct consensus about which way to travel. Devise a plan on how to systematically find your way out. Once decided, the group can send out small scouting teams to test a passage then return and report back their findings.

Caves possess some unique dangers that you should be aware of, including ammonia gas produced by decomposing bat guano. You will probably smell the pungent odor quickly if it's present, and you should turn back unless you have gas masks.

Another danger is from sulfur dioxide, which occurs in geothermally active areas. Sulfur dioxide smells like rotten eggs and can be caustic to your nose, throat, and lungs, especially when mixed with moist air. If you encounter this, turn back.

Jogging

Jogging is fun, and it's good for you. The key to safe jogging is to get into shape slowly. Many beginners lace up their new running shoes and expect to tear up the streets. Forget it. This type of enthusiasm will only get you fatigue, sore muscles, pain, muscle cramps, and maybe even a few sprains.

Before you actually hit the road, you should begin a five- or six-week start-up program consisting of stretching, jogging in place, and a few short excursions. And if you're over thirty-five years old or overweight or generally in poor health, you should have a complete physical examination before starting a running regimen.

Before each jog, warm up slowly, stretching your muscles. Likewise, at the end of each run, cool down slowly and stretch again.

About 60 percent of all runners will sustain an injury

sometime during their running "careers" that keeps them on the sidelines. The majority of these injuries happen to new runners. A good pair of running shoes will go a long way toward keeping your injuries down. Your best advice on which shoes to buy will come from experienced runners.

Aside from muscle strains and sprains, runners also have to cope with other potential hazards, especially cars. Always run facing traffic, and never cross a street without checking both ways. Do the little "at-the-corner jog" while you're looking and waiting for cars.

Avoid running in the ice and snow, and bundle up when it gets cold. There have been cases of frostbite in runners who refused to be intimidated by the falling thermometer. Keep in mind that even if the temperature seems comfortable, evaporating sweat can cool your body and make it seem much colder.

Biking

Each year, about eight hundred people are killed in collisions between bicycles and motor vehicles on roads, and another three hundred bicyclists are killed off the road. More than a million bike riders are injured each year in other accidents.

About a third of bike-related deaths involve children under age fifteen, and three out of four of those deaths are the result of head injuries. Studies have shown that bike helmets can reduce head injuries up to 95 percent for all riders. This is why **the most important factor in bicycle safety is helmets for children and adults.**

Buying a Helmet

When buying a helmet, look for one that is either *Snell* or *ANSI* approved. The requirements of the Snell Memorial Foundation are the most rigorous, and all Snell-approved helmets will have a label inside saying that the helmet has passed the Snell criteria. Requirements for the American National Standards Institute, or ANSI, are also extremely high but not quite as high as Snell's. Either endorsement assures the helmet's efficacy.

Some areas require bike helmets for youngsters. If that's the case, follow the law as to which helmet standard must be met. Some areas insist on Snell while others require ANSI. If no helmets are required, you should at least wear an ANSI helmet. Other helmets that don't meet either of these standards won't give you the protection you need and are not recommended.

SAFETY BY THE NUMBERS

In 1991, there were three fatalities directly related to high school football that involved head injuries.

The most important thing about buying a helmet (aside from the Snell or ANSI standard) is comfort. If a helmet isn't comfortable, you or your child won't wear it. Choose a helmet that fits comfortably and snugly. It should sit level on your head and cover as much as possible. Adjust the straps so the helmet doesn't move around on your head. In fact, no matter how you twist, turn, and pull the helmet, it should not come off if the straps are fastened. Look for buckles that won't come loose easily.

When buying a helmet for your child, choose one that is light. Kids don't like to wear heavy helmets. Also, look for a helmet that is well ventilated. Helmets that are brightly colored make the rider more visible, but resist your child's wish for painting or placing decals and stickers all over the helmet unless they're approved by the manufacturer. Some paints and stickers can degrade the helmet's material.

There is some controversy over hard- versus soft-shelled helmets. In general, the hard shell takes the impact of a fall and disperses the energy; a soft inner lining absorbs the shock. One plus is that if you're thrown from your bike and you slide along the ground, the hard shell won't catch on a corner or curb and jerk your neck. Soft-shell models don't skid as well, and some people contend that the soft shells are good choices for toddlers who can't tolerate a heavier, hard-shell helmet.

In general, however, the hard-shell type is most often recommended and is considered the safest. As for the weight problem, modern materials have brought down the weight of hard-shell helmets to a point where even the smallest toddler probably won't have a problem wearing one.

Clothing

The clothing you wear while riding a bike should also be considered a safety item. Wear brightly colored clothing to make you more visible to cars, pedestrians, and other bicyclists. And if you're riding at night, wear clothing with reflective materials to add safety to your outing. Avoid loose-fitting clothing that can get caught in the bike's moving parts.

The Bicycle

Bicycles must meet minimum safety standards before they can be sold in the United States. They must have reflectors on the front and rear, on the pedals, and on the wheels. Some jurisdictions require additional equipment such as a bell or horn, a white headlight and a red light in back, a basket or rack if you're carrying small packages, and a carrier seat if you're traveling with a small child.

■ A Special Note to Motorists ■

Most bicycle fatalities are the result of collisions between cars and bikes. Many of these fatalities could have been prevented if bicyclists were more careful and obeyed the rules of the road. In addition, motorists should be more careful about bike riders. Here are some tips for motorists on how to deal with bicycles.

- By law, bicycles enjoy the same right of way as a motor vehicle. Of course, bicyclists, especially youngsters, don't always obey the law. In fact, most accidents are caused by bicyclists breaking the law, and that's not fair to you, the motorist. However, if you assume that all cyclists within your view may disregard traffic rules, you could prevent an accident. It's annoying and aggravating at the time, but would you rather yield to a young bike rider or hurt him or her?
- Be alert to bike riders at intersections.

- Look in your side mirror before opening your car door. A bicyclist could be riding by.
- If you're passing a bicyclist who is traveling on the right side of the road, give a light tap on the horn to let him or her know you're there. Don't blast the horn. It could startle the rider and cause him or her to swerve in front of you.
- Don't pass a bike unless you're sure you can do so safely. Bikes can reach high speeds, higher than you might think, especially down hills.

You should consider optional safety equipment for your bicycle, such as a rearview mirror. Many bikers wear small mirrors attached to their helmets or eyeglasses so they can see behind themselves. A visor or eye protection of some kind is always recommended. You'll find that riding a long time can hurt your hands and make the trip uncomfortable, so you should wear gloves to protect your hands from shock and from injuries in case you fall.

Always buy a bike that fits the rider. It's a common mistake to buy a too-big bike for a child, thinking he or she will grow into it. But if you buy a bike that's too big (or too small for that matter) the rider could lose control of it.

Checking the bike for the correct fit is easy. For men's bikes with the horizontal bar, stand with your feet flat on the floor and the bike between your legs. You should have about a half-inch of space between your crotch and the frame tube. For women's bikes without the horizontal bar, subtracting nine inches from your inseam length will give you the correct frame size.

Don't confuse wheel sizes with frame size. Most adult bikes have wheel sizes of twenty-six to twenty-eight inches. The frame size, which is the measurement from the crank axle to the top frame tube, ranges from seventeen to twenty-six inches and has nothing to do with the wheel size.

Always make sure your bike is in good condition before you ride. Check its tires, brakes, chain, gears, and safety equipment. Keep the chain lubricated according to the manufacturer's recommendations.

Rules of the Road

Bike riders must adhere to motor-vehicle laws. For example, you must ride in the same direction as traffic and stop at stop signs. In most areas, bicyclists also are required to use hand signals for turning, yield to pedestrians, and stop for school buses as they load and unload. Bicyclists are normally prohibited from freeways and other controlled-access highways, tunnels, and many bridges.

Bicyclists should also be aware that even though bikes are more maneuverable than cars, they have limitations and special dangers. Be aware of these potential hazards as you ride your bike:

- Motorists don't always see you, so watch for cars leaving driveways and be alert to car doors opening on parked cars in your path.
- Look out for cars, and make eye contact with the driver whenever possible. Let him or her know you're there.
- Watch out for railroad tracks, grates, and storm drains. Cross them slowly at a 90 degree angle.
- Remember that wet leaves can be very slick.
- Roads are most slippery the first moments of a rain shower when the oil comes up from the surface.
- Watch out for sand and gravel on the pavement, and avoid them if you can. If you can't ride around, ride straight through. Don't turn in the middle.
- Always ride single file.
- Don't weave in and out of traffic.
- Pull completely off the road when you stop to rest.
- Learn how to *panic stop*. If you must stop fast, apply both brakes evenly while moving back on the seat and lowering your body. This will keep you from catapulting over the handlebars. As you move back and down, apply greater pressure to the front brake. If you feel the bike skidding, ease off on the front brake.

And one word about headphones: *Don't*. In many states it is against the law for bicyclists to wear headphones while they ride—for good reason. You can't hear what's going on around you if you're concentrating on what's coming out of the headphones. Even if laws in your area allow you to wear headphones while you ride, don't do it. It's dangerous. Some areas prohibit motorists from using headphones too. (Although some states have compromised and permit *one* earphone, it's still not a good idea.)

Skateboarding

Skateboarding is a wonderful sport. It's fun, improves coordination and agility, and it keeps kids away from the TV. It can also be dangerous without the proper equipment.

Seven out of ten skateboard injuries were to children under fifteen years old, according to the Consumer Product Safety Commission. That's not surprising because it's a youngster's sport. Neither is the following statistic surprising: Skateboarders who had been skating less than a week suffered one-third of all reported injuries and riders who have ridden a year or more suffered the next highest number of injuries. In general the new riders suffered injuries due to falls, and experienced riders fell after their boards hit rocks or other debris in the pavement.

What we learn from this set of statistics is: inexperience and irregular surfaces together account for the bulk of skateboarding accidents.

Since nothing can take the place of experience except being on the board, accept the fact that you're going to have some spills while you're getting the hang of it. *Wear protective gear,* including helmets, slip-resistant shoes, wrist braces and gloves, and protection for hips, knees, and elbows. Padded shorts and jackets are also coming on the "thrasher" scene.

Know the surfacing you're going to be riding on. Check it out on foot for holes, cracks, and irregular surfaces. Sweep away debris if necessary. Areas specifically designed for skateboarding are the safest surfaces. Try to use them.

Never ride your skateboard in the street.

Learn how to fall to minimize injury. If you lose your

balance, crouch down so you have less distance to fall. Try to fall on the fleshy parts of your body and then roll. Relax your body instead of going stiff when you hit. Don't land on your hands; you could break your wrists.

Different skateboards are built for different purposes—slalom, freestyle, speed—so be sure to use your board for its intended function.

Winter Recreation

Just because the weather turns cold, it doesn't mean that we should stay indoors. As clothing becomes warmer and more high-tech without adding extra weight, more people are enjoying the wonders of winter sports and recreation. The most popular winter sport is skiing, both cross-country and downhill.

Cross-Country Skiing

Cross-country skiing combines the best parts of being outside with a very beneficial, aerobic exercise. In fact, cross-country skiing is one of the best aerobic exercises available.

You should follow the same suggestions for conditioning, dressing properly, and making sure your equipment is sound for both downhill and cross-country skiing. However, cross-country skiing requires some additional planning and knowledge.

Because people spend a longer time cross-country skiing than downhill skiing—and they're farther from a nice, warm chalet—proper clothing becomes much more important and hypothermia becomes a real possibility.

Never ski beyond your ability. Choose a route you can negotiate without exhaustion. Don't pick a trail that's too long for you, and never be ashamed to turn back if you feel you're going too far. It's no fun if you ski to exhaustion and are a long way home.

Never ski alone, and always tell someone where you're going and when you expect to return. Anticipate delays and factor them into your timetable, but give a realistic estimate as to how long you will be out. Check the weather before you leave and keep an eye out for storms and blizzards. Turn back if you see threatening weather.

■ Windchill ■

We've all heard the expression, "It's not the heat, it's the humidity." If we had a similar expression to describe the cold, it would probably be, "It's not the cold, it's the windchill."

Physicists make the distinction between temperature and cold (to a physicist, cold is not a scientifically correct term. It's really the absence of heat), and so do our bodies. We all know that a temperature of ten degrees Fahrenheit is pretty darn cold, but coupled with a twenty-mile-per-hour wind it feels as if it's twenty-four degrees below zero. What we're talking about is our *perception* of cold as it feels on our bodies. As the wind whips higher, we feel colder. Our physicist friends would say that more heat is being lost from your body as the wind increases. What happens is that the wind blowing against your face whooshes away the thin layer of warmed air surrounding it. This is what's commonly called the *windchill factor* or *windchill effect,* and it's more than a scientist's term. Windchill is real and it's dangerous.

Even if you're dressed warmly enough to withstand, say, zero degrees, if the wind kicks up you could become a victim of hypothermia or even frostbite. So, before you head out into the cold, don't just look at the thermometer. Check the wind forecast as well.

Be prepared for bad weather and delays beyond your control by carrying spare clothing and food. Learn how to camp in cold weather. Sometimes it's safer to bivouac and rest for the night than trying to get home in the dark or in a storm.

All cross-country skiers should be proficient at reading maps and compasses. Attach your compass to your clothes with a cord so it won't get lost, and keep your map handy for reference. Before you begin your trip, go over your route on the map. Make sure you know where you're going. Every member of your group should have a map and a compass and know how to use them.

If you're traveling in a new area, get advice from local

cross-country skiers about the terrain and weather conditions. Each area is unique, and there's no way for you to know about its particular quirks if you're from out of town.

Downhill Skiing

It's no secret that downhill skiing is dangerous. Almost everyone knows someone who has had a skiing accident. About 100,000 skiers each year suffer some injury ranging from minor cuts to serious dislocations. Most skiing injuries are caused by falls, and the most common injuries are cuts, bruises, and twisting of legs and ankles. No surprises there, but what's interesting (although again, not surprising) is that most injuries occur to people who have never skied before and they're on their first day out.

Skiers who are in good condition have fewer accidents, so avoiding accidents means getting into shape both physically and mentally. Even if you do fall, you will hurt yourself less if you're in good physical condition. That goes for every sport, not just skiing. Getting in shape means doing exercises that build your stamina, strength, agility, and flexibility. Not only will this prevent accidents but it will also help you enjoy skiing more because your muscles won't ache after the first day. Don't start exercising the day before you go skiing. Instead, plan well in advance, weeks or months if you can. You'll be better off for the effort.

Warming up on site also will help you have a safer skiing time. Athletes who warm themselves up before their sport always do better and suffer fewer injuries. Don't forget to stretch before you start skiing. In addition, start slowly, maybe trying a few beginner, or "bunny," trails before trying the bigger slopes. *Don't take on more hill than you can handle.* Skiing beyond your level is one of the prime factors in accidents. The same goes for showing off, or "hotdogging."

Take lessons from a professional instructor. The pro will not only teach you how to ski but also how to avoid accidents. Moreover, the pro will know the area and he or she can steer you away from trouble spots or tricky areas. Pros can also assess your skills and point you toward slopes that are commensurate with your abilities.

It sounds like common sense, but make sure you're dressed properly for the weather. The ultra-bright sun in ski areas should not fool you into believing it's warmer than it really is. Don't wear jeans and sweaters. They can get wet from the snow and your own sweat, then they freeze. Instead, wear layers of thermal underwear, waterproof gloves and pants, and a hat. They keep you warm and dry.

Always wear tinted goggles. Not only do they prevent injury to your eyes from flying snow and ice but they keep you from suffering snow blindness. After spending a day on the ski slopes with the sun reflecting off the snow, it may take some time for you to get your normal vision back, especially if you're going to drive at night. And don't forget to wear sun block.

All bindings should be in good working condition; they should disengage properly. Make sure you test them before you ski.

A few accidents occur on lift chairs and T-bars, and you should be mindful of the potential for loose clothing, especially scarves, to get caught. Fortunately, most injuries are averted in this area by alert operators who keep a pretty careful eye on the lifts.

Avalanche

Avalanches are caused by snow crystals that have not had time or the proper conditions to bond together into a stable, cohesive snowpack. As a result, any disturbance such as noise or vibration can cause some areas of snow to fall and take more snow with it.

Sometimes avalanches are gentle, just a little snow sliding down the hill. Other times, however, avalanches can reach speeds of more than seventy-five miles an hour and rampage down a mountain, crushing everything in its path. Some avalanches are so large and powerful that a pocket of air proceeds the snow and causes damage to houses, trees, and anything else in its path. Whatever was in the way of the avalanche is buried under many feet of snow.

There is little danger to skiers who ski at resorts with maintained slopes. Most resorts have avalanche patrols searching for areas with avalanche conditions. These patrols either rope avalanche areas to keep them "off limits" or use explosives to trigger small avalanches before they become big and dangerous.

Skiers who venture beyond the resort's designated ski areas face avalanche dangers. If you're thinking about going off the beaten track, check with local authorities about avalanche conditions. Many areas have warning centers that rank the chance of avalanches much the same way the Coast Guard ranks wind and wave conditions in its small-craft advisories.

In general, avalanches occur less often on less steep slopes. Hills with an incline of less than thirty degrees don't usually host avalanches. In addition, the south side of slopes, which get the most sunlight, also have fewer avalanches because the sun's heat melts the snow and allows it to bond tightly.

Even if you're a cross-country skier at the bottom of the hill, not a downhill skier on the mountain itself, you would be wise to keep away from any hills with avalanche potential.

Serious Weather

Everyone talks about the weather, but nobody does anything about it. That funny, old saying might be outdated one day. Meteorologists and other scientists are studying ways to prevent a devastating tornado or bring rain to farmland hit by drought might. One day they might just be able to "do something" about serious weather. For now, however, we must be content with predicting the weather as best as we can and taking the appropriate precautions.

Meteorologists have made great strides in recent years in predicting weather. These forecasts can often give us the advance warning we need to prevent damage to our homes and loss of lives—providing we know what to do.

This discussion is geared toward those most immediately concerned by weather: people who live in areas that experience violent weather and those of us who spend a lot of time outdoors. That's why it's here in the chapter on recreation.

Tornadoes

Most parts of the country aren't concerned about tornadoes. But there's a swath of land in the central United States that stretches across the prairies from Iowa to Texas called "Tornado Alley" where conditions frequently favor these violent twisters. When tornadoes are forming, they need unencumbered land to build up power and this area provides that open land.

Tornado Alley is not only the most common area in the United States for tornadoes, it's the most prolific tornado region in the world. Three-quarters of the world's major tornadoes occur here. Tornadoes form mostly in May, June, and April (in that order) and there are very few in the winter months. Most tornadoes occur between noon and midnight, with the bulk occurring in the late afternoon between four and six.

Tornadoes cause more injuries (but not deaths) than any other weather condition, mainly from falling debris. The twisters do their damage in two ways: First, the winds that can reach 150 to 300 miles per hour can turn over cars and uproot trees. Second, the vacuum inside the funnel can pick up homes and drop them like dollhouses. In addition, the vacuum can also cause a great difference in the outside and inside pressure of a building and cause it to implode.

SAFETY BY THE NUMBERS

On average, almost one hundred deaths are due to tornadoes each year in the United States.

The National Weather Service (NWS) has two tornado alerts:

Tornado Watch, issued when conditions are favorable for a tornado.

Tornado Warning, issued when a tornado or group of tornadoes has actually been sighted.

Along with the watch or warning, the NWS gives instructions on precautions to take. These steps include:

- Keep listening to the radio and television to receive the latest information
- Watch the skies for funnel-shaped clouds or sudden, violent winds and rain.
- If you're in open country where you can't find shelter, such as a golf course, lie flat in the nearest depression or ditch.
- In the mall: Go to the designated shelter. Don't try to drive away.
- In your home: If you have a basement, go there. If not, stay in the lowest part of the structure. Take shelter underneath sturdy furniture or in a closet or bathroom. The idea is that if your house gets hit, you won't be struck by flying debris. Turn off all electrical power and gas to your house. This will help prevent fire if your home is damaged.
- In school: Avoid rooms with large, high-vaulted ceilings. Go to the basement if your school has one.
- Mobile homes: Leave the mobile home immediately. These structures are notorious for sustaining tornado damage. Hide in a ditch or depression.
- In your car: If a tornado is heading your way, don't try to outdrive it. Get out of your car and hide in a low spot. Some of the safest areas are under steel-reinforced concrete highway underpasses.

Floods

Flash floods cause more deaths in the United States than any other weather condition. One reason for their terrible toll is that people often underestimate the awesome power and swiftness of water. Even people driving in their cars can be tooling along one minute and surrounded by roof-high water the next. Quick, intense rainfalls in a very small area can cause flash flooding. So can a longer-lasting hurricane or many days of steady rain.

Either way, the result is the same. Streams and rivers in the area are unable to handle the amount of rainfall—their banks overflow—and the resulting wall of water can often reach twenty feet high and move in excess of twenty miles an hour.

Ground that is frozen or already saturated from previous rains can also be a factor. Flash floods even occur in the desert where the water from a freak storm cannot be absorbed by the dry, packed sand or dirt. The condition is exacerbated in desert areas that are built up with residential or industrial construction and contain many parking lots (Las Vegas comes to mind). These hard-surfaced areas only serve to increase runoff with little opportunity for the ground to absorb water.

There is no way you can fight a flash flood. The only thing you can do is to head for higher ground.

The National Weather Service has two flash-flood alerts:

Flash-Flood Watch, issued when streams are expected to overflow from a sudden downpour or from melting snow or ice. In the latter case, you may have several days' notice of this, and forecasters can often predict with good certainty when a specific stream or river will crest or reach its maximum height.

Flash-Flood Warning, may be issued during a downpour, giving you only minutes to escape.

Follow these suggestions for keeping yourself and your family safe during floods:

- Know in advance where you would head in case of flooding.
- If you're driving in your car when a flash-flood warning is issued, immediately head toward high ground. Be careful of bridges, tunnels, and low spots in the road. Remember, a sudden flood on the road could toss your car like a toy.
- If your car becomes stalled in a low area, leave it and escape immediately on foot.
- Don't attempt to cross streams or rivers on foot.
- Don't climb on your roof or in trees hoping to escape the floods except as a last resort.
- Turn off all gas and electrical power to your house.

After the flood:

- If your home was flooded, have a trained person check your appliances for water damage before you turn them on again.
- Be aware that sewage systems may back up and taint the water with bacteria and other diseases. Make sure you throw out any food that is suspect.
- Don't drink any water until it's been checked by your local health agency.

Hurricanes

About the only thing positive you can say for hurricanes is that you usually have ample warning. Forecasting technology has become so good that meteorologists can pretty well tell where a hurricane is going and the expected magnitude of the winds and rain. However, nature doesn't follow a schedule and hurricanes do change course and intensity, but in most cases you will have a chance to protect your life and property.

Hurricane season is fairly predictable. In the United States, these massive storms occur from June through November, with most of them occurring in September. The average hurricane lasts about nine days with most of its "life" spent over water, where it forms and gains strength before hitting land.

The typical hurricane has average winds of one hundred miles per hour and drops an average of six to twelve inches of water a day. Although the winds cause great damage, hurricanes also cause *storm surges* a rapid rise in tide levels that flood coastal areas. The storms tend to lose power once they're over land.

The National Weather Service has a system of alerts for hurricanes too:

Hurricane Advisory: This means that a tropical depression, or low-pressure area, is forming and could come together to form a hurricane. Sometimes they form, and sometimes they fall apart. Stay alert.

Hurricane Watch: The land within this area faces possible danger from a hurricane within twenty-four hours. Again, the storm system could fall apart or form and change direction and head back out to sea.

Hurricane Warning: This means a hurricane is heading for your area. You should proceed with your hurricane contingency plans.

Before the storm season even begins, make sure you have the proper emergency items if you live in a hurricane area: flashlight, portable radio, extra batteries, nonperishable foods, tools, boards for windows.

Be familiar with the official evacuation route in your jurisdiction. Know how long it will take you to reach a safe area.

Take these safety measure just prior to the storm:

- Board up windows on your house and move cars out of danger. (Always keep your car fueled and ready during hurricane season.)
- Secure all patio furniture or anything in your yard that could be blown by the wind. This includes garbage cans and garden knickknacks.
- Secure your boat or take it out of the area.
- If you're going to stay in your home, make sure it's on high ground and strong enough to withstand the winds and rain. Once the storm starts, don't go outside.
- Don't be fooled into thinking the storm is over if the eye passes over your area. You may have a few minutes to a half-hour of calm, but the winds will whip up again with the same intensity as before although from the opposite direction. Take care of emergency repairs outside, but come inside at the first sign of increased wind.
- If you're not going to stay at home, head for the nearest designated shelter. Stay there until the authorities deem it safe to leave. Remember: most shelters will not allow you to bring animals. Be sure you have plans for their safety too.

Take these safety measures after the storm:
- Be careful of fallen power lines and wire. Don't touch!

- If your house has been damaged extensively, wait until it can be checked by an inspector before entering.
- Don't drink any water until it's been checked by the health department.
- If your power has been off, make sure food in the refrigerator and freezer are still safe to eat. If frozen food has thawed, throw it away.
- Stay away from streams and rivers. Flash flooding could occur.
- Continue to listen to the radio for information.
- Be careful when driving. The storm may have undermined the supporting material under roadways. Be wary of bridges and areas where rocks have fallen onto the road.

Lightning

Summer months are the most dangerous for lightning deaths: July has the highest number of lightning-related fatalities, followed by August and June. Of the average ninety-four deaths annually attributed to lightning, about two-thirds occur during these months, according to the National Safety Council. People who are outdoors in open areas are susceptible to lightning strikes. Those inside, even in their cars, rarely have anything to fear from lightning.

SAFETY BY THE NUMBERS

In 1990, 125,000 volleyball injuries were reported in U.S. hospital emergency rooms.

Lightning occurs as the result of a difference in electrical potential between two areas, such as a cloud and the earth. Lightning isn't limited to cloud-to-earth strikes. It can also be seen striking from cloud to cloud and from cloud to water.

Although lightning strikes are swift, you may have some warning. First, lightning usually accompanies storm clouds and storms and it rarely "strikes out of the blue," despite the cliché. Second, lightning survivors have reported a tingling just prior to a strike. Some say their hair stood up and their skin felt electrically charged.

This happens because lightning strikes are actually two strikes. In the case of cloud-to-ground, one goes up (or down) and sort of clears the path (technically speaking, it ionizes the route) for the main strike to follow. The first strike is very weak, so when you see a lightning strike you're really seeing half of the entire process, albeit the powerful part. The tingling that people feel just before the strike is that first and minor strike.

Lightning will take the path of least resistance, which in some cases could be your body. It's easier for lightning to pass through you on its way to the ground than through another six feet of air. This is the theory behind lightning rods: if you place an easily traveled route for lightning to follow—such as a metal rod on your house connected to the ground with thick cable—it will take that route instead of going through your house. For the rod to be effective, it should form a protective zone around your house that is determined by drawing a forty-five-degree cone from the top of the rod to the ground. If your house is inside that area, it will be protected.

Always run for cover as soon as you see threatening weather. Don't take chances. Follow these suggestions for additional safety:

- If you're in a flat area with no opportunity for cover, lie flat. If you see a ravine or low area, hide there.
- Keep off mountaintops and high ridges.
- Cars are excellent insulators, provided you stay inside and don't touch the auto's doors or other parts. Sit in the middle of the seat.
- Hiding under a small group of trees may be safe if there are other, larger trees nearby. Don't hide under very tall or isolated trees.
- Don't hide in a cave or rock depression inside a mountain or hillside unless it's very deep—not just an overhang—and you can walk back inside. Keep away from the walls.
- If possible, lie on insulating material such a blanket, coiled rope, or sleeping bag.
- Avoid sitting on wet rocks and moss.

Lightning can injure you in two ways. The direct lightning strike itself, which is high-voltage electricity, can damage your nervous system and attack your heart and brain, causing almost instantaneous death. The other, more common hazard is an indirect hit that occurs when lightning strikes near you. If, for example, you're near a tree that is hit by lightning, you may suffer severe burns from sparks and heat. There is also some electricity in the ground that can injure you, although not as severely as if you sustained a direct hit. And yes, in case you're wondering, lightning can indeed strike twice in the same spot.

Blizzards

Blizzards are winter storms that drop lots of snow in a very short time. The main danger from blizzards is when you're driving in an isolated area and the snow drifts so high and so fast that you can't drive anymore. You're stranded, and it's cold.

Studies have shown that the majority of drivers caught in blizzards knew they were taking a chance—knew a storm was coming—but decided to take the risk.

■ Weather Radios ■

Without a doubt, your best source of information about pending weather is from the National Oceanic and Atmospheric Administration's (NOAA) network of stations.

These stations transmit the most up-to-date weather information twenty-four hours a day. Unfortunately, you can't pick up these stations on your regular AM or FM radio. You'll need either a police-scanner radio or a *weather radio* designed just to pick up these stations.

Weather radios can be bought in many department or variety stores as well as stores that sell stereos, TVs, and other electrical appliances. The cost is usually twenty dollars and up. (For you radio buffs, the frequencies are 162.400, 162.425, 162.450, 162.475, 162.500, 162.525 and 162.55 megahertz.)

The advantage of these weather radios is that they often have a feature that keeps the radio silent unless a special alert tone is sent to indicate a weather emergency exists. It is followed by a special broadcast warning of severe weather. Of course, any time you want to listen to the radio for regular weather broadcasts—without an existing emergency condition—it's available.

The NOAA stations have a range of about twenty-five to fifty miles, and every part of the country is within range of at least one station. The information is customized, depending upon the region. Coastal-area stations offer marine forecasts, and farm-area stations give agricultural outlooks. Most marine two-way radios can receive these stations, and many police-scanner radios have controls for quick access to these stations as well.

The best advice is obvious: don't drive if you know a storm is on the way. However, if you get stranded by an unexpected storm, stay with your car. Run the engine periodically to heat the inside, but try to preserve gas because you don't know how long the storm will last. Be sure to open the window a crack so you don't succumb to carbon monoxide poisoning.

If you run out of gas, close all the windows and stuff any cracks or openings (the gas and brake pedal areas for instance) with anything you can find. Cold is your enemy, so try to keep warm with extra hats, scarves, or whatever you can find in the car. Don't leave your car unless you're absolutely, positively sure that shelter is very close by. Even then, wait until the blizzard stops before trying to reach it. Deep snow is one thing, but fighting the wind and snow is more tiring than you might think.

If you live in an area where blizzards are common, keep an emergency kit in your home and car. The kit should include extra outerwear, nonperishable food, and a jug of water. You might also want to consider a phone for your car or CB radios for your house and car if you live and travel in an isolated area.

After the blizzard, keep away from downed power lines and trees that are creaking under the snow's weight. Check the roof of your house for signs of damage from the snow.

The Last Word on Sports

We didn't discuss the hazards of sports like baseball, basketball, golf, or hockey in this chapter because common sense and the following rules should be enough for most casual players or those on organized teams. (Do we really have to tell you to duck when you hear someone on the golf course scream "Fore!"?)

SAFETY BY THE NUMBERS

In 1990, there were thirty reported parachuting fatalities.

If you already play these sports, you've probably heard these suggestions before, but it never hurts to be reminded:

- Never play sports without the proper equipment, and that includes correct shoes for the sport.
- Never roughhouse beyond what the sport allows. (Hear that, hockey players?)
- Always pay attention to your coach's instructions and obey them.
- Never play if you're tired from lack of sleep, overwork, or prescription drugs.
- Never push an injury. If you hurt your leg, sit out the rest of the game.
- Most important: **wear eye protection.** Whatever the sport—tennis, racquet ball, hockey, basketball, soccer—wherever a projectile is involved or body contact takes place, you should wear eye protection. Nearly one-third of all sports-related eye injuries occur to children age five to fourteen, and about ninety-six thousand eye injuries occur on school playing fields alone. These injuries range from mild irritations and "black eyes" to blindness. If you wear prescription glasses, be particularly careful as your eyes may be injured by the impact of your glasses and frames being thrust into your eyes. You should wear sports prescription eye guards available from your optician. Soccer, which is becoming very popular in the United States, is also responsible for many eye injuries because part of the game is to hit the ball with your head.

CHAPTER

Food Safety

YOU EAT TO live, but you also take a calculated risk whenever you eat because it's impossible to eat foods that are guaranteed to be 100 percent safe.

Modern food-handling processes often exacerbate this problem. Because time is money, food processors have been known to sacrifice cleanliness for swiftness and efficiency. In addition, with most of our food no longer locally produced, locally processed, and locally eaten, there is greater opportunity for our food to be contaminated before it reaches our table.

But even with all the horror stories about contaminated food we've heard in recent years, our food supply is still quite sanitary and healthy although it's not quite as good as in some European and Scandinavian countries, where governments play a more aggressive inspection role. On the other hand, the United States food supply is certainly more sanitary than most nations'.

While we, as individuals, have little control over how our food is handled before it reaches us, we have a great deal of control after we buy it. We also have choices as to what kinds of foods we're going to buy. By taking certain steps, we may be able to counteract or eliminate some of the harm done to food by the producer, processor, shipper, and retailer. In addition, by using precautions, we can prevent food from becoming contaminated due to our own storage, handling, and preparation methods. Interestingly, the U.S. Food and Drug

Administration estimates that 30 percent of all food-borne illnesses are the result of improper food handling at home.

What Makes Us Sick?

For the most part, bacteria cause food-related illnesses.
These bacteria range from staphylococcal, which causes diar-
rhea, cramps, and nausea but is rarely fatal, to botulism toxin,
which causes neurological symptoms such as double vision
and speech difficultly and can be fatal if not treated.

All cases of food poisoning should be considered dangerous. All instances of possible food poisoning should be
watched carefully and treated with respect, based on your
symptoms and your past experience. (Who among us hasn't
eaten something "bad" that gave us food poisoning for a
short time, but we were fine a few hours later?) If you have
food poisoning, try to remember what you ate and where you
ate it. If you go to your doctor, this information could help his
or her diagnosis. For most cases of food poisoning requiring
medical attention, antibiotics are prescribed to help destroy
the bacteria.

We should also mention that food poisoning can be
caused by viruses. One of the most serious is hepatitis A,
which is found in mollusks and shellfish that were infected by
untreated sewage in their habitats or in any food contaminated by human feces. The hepatitis virus is treatable, but
early medical attention is crucial as hepatitis can lead to liver
damage and even death. There is no actual cure for hepatitis,
but there are treatments that can help the body fight off the
virus. Also, some medicines can prevent damage to bodily
organs from the virus while the body is healing.

Safe Food Buying

Food safety starts in the supermarket, so choose your
food store carefully. Check the store for general cleanliness. Is
it free of dirt and insects? Are workers who deal with unpack-
aged food, (in the deli section, for instance) wearing hats (if

required,) clean clothes, and gloves? Are they careful to keep cooked fish, meat, and poultry separate from raw fish, meat and poultry?

Do they wash their hands or change to fresh gloves when handling cooked food after handling uncooked food? Is the cutting counter clean? Are nonfood items such as glass cleaners kept away from the area? You'll find that most supermarkets have established safe food-handling procedures and equipment, but it's up to each employee to obey the rules.

Check the thermometers on the meat and dairy refrigerator shelves for the proper temperature. Most stores have their thermometers marked for the correct range. Be sure the needle is there.

Local health authorities check food stores for cleanliness, and a record of their report should be public record. In most areas, it must be displayed in the store. Look for it.

Buying food requires care too. When you buy canned goods, don't buy any cans that are cracked, dented, or bulging. Pay attention to expiration dates. **Never buy outdated food.**

For packaged products such as pasta and breads, also look at the expiration dates. Check the "buy by" and "use by" dates. Pick foods that will last the longest in your house. If the package is clear, check all sides of the product for any damage, dirt, or mold.

Buy produce with rinds or skins that are free from dents, bruises, and cracks. Are vegetables stored in cool zones when necessary? Are fruits restocked to cool shelves as soon as possible, or are they stored in boxes in the aisles longer than necessary?

Always buy your frozen and refrigerated foods last. Place all frozen foods (or very cold foods) in plastic bags so their drippings don't contaminate other foods. If you've got a long trip home, especially in hot weather, bring a cooler to carry the frozen items.

Make sure eggs have been refrigerated in the store. Before buying them, check each egg for cracks and leaks. Dismiss the entire dozen if you see a leaking egg. It could contaminate the ones next to it.

When shopping for meat, make sure it is very cold or

frozen. Check packages for leakage. Sometimes supermarkets make old meat more attractive by placing parsley or other garnish in the package. Beware of old meat that's been "dressed up" in this manner.

The same rules apply to buying poultry. It's becoming popular for supermarkets to sell poultry that is "fresh chilled" or "chill packed." This means the bird has been quickly chilled and kept at temperatures ranging from twenty-eight to thirty-two degrees. The poultry is not quite frozen but kept cold enough to keep bacteria growth in check. Poultry that is kept in this manner can be cooked as if it were fresh, or you can freeze it for later. Birds sold in this manner may have some ice crystals and "give" a little when you press it.

When buying shellfish, check thoroughly for signs of contamination. **Never buy cooked shellfish that has been displayed in the same case as raw fish.** The raw fish can contaminate the cooked shellfish. Shells of clams, mollusks, and oysters should be closed, or they should close when they're tapped. Necks of steamer clams should twitch when their shells are tapped. Fresh crabs should move when you touch them, and fresh lobsters should curl their tails when you pick them up.

When buying other fish, look at their eyes. They should be clear—except in a few species such as walleye pike—and only bulge a little. Flesh should be firm. Touch the fish. If it doesn't bounce back, if your finger leaves an indentation, don't buy it.

Perhaps the best method for checking the freshness of fish is the smell test. **If fish smells bad, it probably is. Rinse it first under cold water, then let your nose at it. Fish should not smell, well,** *fishy*. Sometimes fish smells like ammonia. This could be a sign of spoilage, or the fish could have absorbed ammonia gas from a leaking refrigerator (industrial freezers sometimes use ammonia as a coolant). Either way, don't buy it.

When purchasing frozen fish, select packages that are not opened or damaged. Look for clear packages that allow you to see the fish inside. If you see frost or ice crystals, it could mean that the fish has been stored for a long time or thawed and refrozen.

Safe Food Handling

Consumers have the most control over the safety of their food in the areas of storage and preparation. Because each type of food requires unique techniques for handling, it's easiest to discuss foods individually. As you'll see in the following pages, handling meats is very different than handling vegetables.

SAFETY BY THE NUMBERS

About 30 percent of all food-borne illnesses are the result of improper handling at home, according to the F.D.A.

Eggs

Store eggs in your refrigerator in the original carton if possible (this keeps them from breaking or cracking from handling). Store them no higher than forty degrees Fahrenheit. Do not wash eggs; they've already been washed.

Use fresh eggs within five weeks and hard-boiled eggs within one week. If you've separated whites and yolks, you should use them as soon as possible, within a few hours. Always wash your hands with hot soapy water after you've handled raw eggs. The same goes for utensils and countertops.

Serve egg dishes hot and immediately after cooking. If you want to save cooked eggs, put them in the refrigerator immediately and use them within three days.

In the past few years, we've seen the rise of salmonella incidents in persons eating raw or undercooked eggs. In fact, legislators in the state of New Jersey considered a ban on serving runny eggs in restaurants. Avoid eating raw eggs, and make sure all eggs are cooked thoroughly to kill any bacteria. Remember that raw eggs are often served in Caesar salads and steak tartare. Lightly cooked eggs are also found in some custards, meringues, and French toast. Commercial versions of mayonnaise and eggnog are usually made with eggs that have been pasteurized to kill bacteria.

Meats

When you arrive home, immediately store meats in the coldest part of your refrigerator, usually the lowest level, or in the freezer. Some refrigerators have drawers especially designed for meat. The refrigerator temperature for safe meat storage is thirty-five to forty degrees Fahrenheit and zero degrees for freezers. Fresh meats only last a few days in the refrigerator. Freeze them if you won't use them soon, but note that the freezer in most home refrigerator-freezers doesn't go as low as zero. A separate freezer might go to zero, and it is recommended for long-term storage. Store meat in its original plastic wrap from the supermarket or in plastic or paper while in the refrigerator. In the freezer, wrap meats in moisture-proof freezer wrap. "Freezer burn" is caused by drying out of meat. It's not harmful, but "burned" meat has lost flavor.

Thaw frozen meat in the refrigerator—it could take about twenty-four hours—never outside on a counter. Room-temperature defrosting can lead to bacteria production. To thaw meat quickly, put it under running cold water or in your microwave. Keep luncheon meats in their original wrapping in the refrigerator until you use them, then rewrap them tightly. Freezing is not a good idea.

Always use hot, soapy water to wash your hands, utensils, dishes, countertops, or anything else that touches raw meat. Never put cooked meat on a dish that held raw meat, and never use the same cooking utensil for raw and cooked meat without washing it first. This is especially important when you barbecue because there is a tendency to bring a plate of raw meat outside then use that same dish to carry in your cooked items.

Cook all meat thoroughly. If you like your meat very rare, or raw in the case of steak tartare, realize that you're taking a risk. As we have learned in recent years, food inspections by federal agencies have been less than adequate.

■ Food-Preparation Basics ■

1. Always wash your hands with hot, soapy water before you handle food.
2. Wash all utensils, dishes, plates, and cutting boards before using them.
3. Plastic or glass cutting boards are less likely to hold bacteria in crevasses and knife cuts than wooden cutting boards.
4. Never let raw meats, fish, or poultry touch already-cooked foods either directly or through your hands, utensils, dishes. and cutting boards.
5. Never thaw anything at room temperature. Thaw it in the refrigerator or in cool running water or water that is changed every thirty minutes. Once it's thawed, cook it immediately.
6. After preparation, keep hot food hot (140 degrees or above) and cold food cold (45 degrees or below). Never let hot foods cool down to room temperature. Place them in the refrigerator until you're ready to eat, and reheat if necessary. A safe temperature for reheating most food is about 165 degrees Fahrenheit.
7. "Listen" to your nose. Never eat any food that smells spoiled (although a normal smell is not a guarantee that the food is not spoiled.)

Just because the Department of Agriculture stamp appears on meat does not mean the meat is free of bacteria. Inspectors generally engage in visual checks of meats, but they have no way of knowing whether bacteria lurks in the carcasses that have passed their inspection station. In addition, not all pieces of meat receive individual visual inspections. Often, inspectors spot-check large lots of meat. This means individual carcasses escape inspection.

A good rule of thumb is that meats should be cooked to a temperature of 140 degrees Fahrenheit (pork to 150 degrees) to ensure that bacteria have been destroyed. Use a meat thermometer to verify the temperature.

Refrigerate leftovers immediately; bacteria can grow quickly on cooling food. It's a good idea to cut meat into slices so it will cool rapidly in the refrigerator. Wrap it to keep air out.

Poultry

No food item has received more attention lately than poultry. Because of its low price, low fat, and high nutritional value, poultry has become extremely popular. Along with that popularity, though, has come news that the poultry industry may be less sanitary than we would like. Again, inspectors are not fully checking carcasses for bacteria and disease as the number of processed chickens and turkeys increases.

Quick-chilled poultry should be stored in its original store wrapper, or you can rewrap it loosely in your own wrap. Always place it on a plate to prevent juices from dripping and contaminating other food. The ideal temperature for poultry storage is twenty-eight to thirty-two degrees, lower than the usually thirty-five to forty degrees that most home refrigerators are kept. It's best to use poultry within two days of purchase. Fresh poultry can be kept a little longer in your refrigerator if it is unopened. If you buy poultry rock-solid frozen, you may freeze it or let it thaw in your refrigerator for use. Follow the directions on the package.

Thawing is a little tricky for poultry because we're sometimes dealing with large items. For example, it can take four to five days for a twenty-five-pound turkey to thaw. If you need to thaw it faster, use the cold-water method or try the microwave oven. Most frozen turkeys come with detailed thawing instructions.

It bears repeating: **never thaw frozen meats, poultry, or fish at room temperature. This is the ideal condition in which bacteria can grow.**

Cook poultry according to the instructions on the package, usually to 165 degrees Fahrenheit. Always cook it until all the pink color is gone. Never eat pink poultry flesh; it may not be cooked thoroughly. In addition, always cook the entire bird at once.

Always clean the stuffing cavity well, according to instructions, and never stuff poultry until you're ready to cook it.

Fish

There's a cliché about gambling: "You pays your money and you takes your chances." It's not flip to say that the same cliché could apply to eating some shellfish. Although the number of illnesses from eating cooked mollusks such as clams, oysters, and mussels is actually lower than for eating poultry—one illness per million servings compared with one illness for every twenty-five thousand servings of poultry—the risk rises when we're talking about raw shellfish. According to the Food and Drug Administration, one out of every one thousand to two thousand servings of raw shellfish makes someone ill.

When you think about it, the reason is obvious. Mollusks live (and sometimes move) by filtering water through their systems, and in so doing, they ingest harmful bacteria and virus from their surroundings. Many of these bacteria and viruses come from raw sewage and industrial waste dumped by people. While this may not have been a problem before the growth of industry, it is now.

Now add to that the fact that we eat these little creatures completely, including their digestive systems which contain a concentration of bacteria and viruses, and you can see why there's a problem with eating raw mollusks.

SAFETY BY THE NUMBERS

About 85 percent of illnesses caused by eating seafood are the result of eating raw oysters, clams, and mollusks, says the F.D.A.

Several states even require signs where shellfish is sold, warning customers that eating raw shellfish can cause serious illness in persons with liver, stomach, blood, or immune disorders. In 1991, the Food and Drug Administration created a new Office of Seafood to oversee the group's seafood-safety programs. Until this office was established, seafood inspections were not done by the federal government. It's too early to judge the office's effectiveness, but the United States is still very far behind most other industrialized nations when it comes to seafood inspection.

The most important thing you can do to protect yourself against diseases in shellfish is not to eat them raw.

For those who simply *must* have raw shellfish, cold weather months are said to be safer times to eat them because the shellfish are less likely to be carrying bacteria and viruses. Always buy from a seafood store that is clean and inspected by local health agencies. Beware of roadside stands without the proper storage or sanitary conditions. It's important to deal with reputable seafood dealers who buy only from fishermen who adhere to local rules and regulations about fishing areas that are off-limits. Because it's more expensive to fish far from shore where the waters are less polluted, shellfish caught in close-in, off-limits areas are often cheaper. Be wary of low shellfish prices.

Store live shellfish in the refrigerator, and keep them damp with a wet towel or cloth. Do not place them on ice or immerse them in fresh water, and never place fresh shellfish in an airtight container. The goal is to keep shellfish alive until you cook them. Lobsters and crabs will stay alive in the refrigerator using the damp-cloth method for about twenty-four hours.

Oysters and clams should be placed in boiling water and cooked for four to six minutes at full boil. Alternatively, you can steam them for six to eight minutes. Boiling other shellfish will also kill bacteria and viruses.

SAFETY BY THE NUMBERS

According to the F.D.A., about one in one million servings of seafood will make someone ill—if you don't include raw mollusks.

As for cooking other seafood, fish doesn't take long, usually a few minutes on each side depending upon the thickness. Whether you fry, boil, or bake fish, it's usually done when it flakes easily with a fork and is no longer translucent.

Fruits and Vegetables

Fruits and vegetables should be refrigerated as soon as you get them home. Some people do leave their fruit out, but that's generally not a good idea especially in warm weather because fruits attract insects.

Always check fruit before you buy it, and do not buy any fruit or vegetable with holes because insects may have burrowed in. The main danger from fruits and vegetables is from pesticides and insecticides. While all U.S. growers are bound to obey the law and only use government-approved chemicals, this may not be true for foreign growers. If you have any doubts about where your produce is grown, ask the store's produce manager.

Wash all fruit and vegetables with a brush *before* you cut into the skin.

CHAPTER **8**

A Primer on Baby Safety

MOBILE, EXPLORING CHILDREN present their parents with a great challenge—letting them explore, yet keeping them accident-free.

Accept the fact that all children will have accidents at one time or another. Some, because of their inquisitive, active nature, will have more than others. Most kids will jump off the couch at least once in their lives when you're not looking. There's not much you can do about it.

As parents, the best you can do is try to limit some of these accidents and their severity by *childproofing* your house and yard. You may not be able to keep your child from showing interest in what's inside a cabinet, but you can definitely keep him or her from opening it and getting at the dangerous cleaning chemicals inside.

Childproofing should suit your child's maturity. When a child is just learning to walk and reach, he or she doesn't always understand the word no. As the child gets older, he or she will understand which areas to be careful in, and your childproofing should reflect that. On the other hand, depending upon your disciplinary techniques and your child's nature, the best thing might be to just get everything out of the child's way and lock up everything that's dangerous.

While this book isn't a treatise on child-rearing, it must be said that childproofing should never be a substitute for discipline and teaching a child how to respect hazardous items and materials and use them in a safe manner.

The Kitchen

Let's start in the kitchen, the site of most accidents. As you look around the room, see the dangers from a child's perspective and think in the child's terms, saying, "Hmmm, what can I grab now?" There's nothing more enticing to a small child than something sticking out.

With that in mind, here are some more suggestions for childproofing your kitchen:

- Turn all handles from pots and pans away from the outside of the counter. Don't give a child the opportunity to grab a handle from a hot pot or pan. Consider using an oven guard that will keep your child from reaching the top of the oven door.
- Never leave cookies or other treats near or above the stove. Don't give your child a reason to climb on the stove.
- Lock all cabinets that contain household chemicals.
- Lock drawers that contain knives and other sharp objects.
- Don't place any glass or heavy containers on counters where a child can reach for them. The same goes for knives and other sharp objects; push them back from the edge.
- Once your child starts to climb, don't leave your step stool out where he or she can use it as a stepping-stone to the countertop.
- Be mindful of dog and cat food that's on the floor. Children will be attracted to it because they see the pet eating it. Dry dog or cat food won't poison your child, but he or she may choke on the pieces and also get a stomach ache. Canned pet food made of meat can go bad if left out. While it may not affect your pet, there have been cases of children eating dog food that harbored salmonella bacteria.

- Never let appliance cords hang off the counter.
- Never leave hot dishes or containers of hot liquids where your child can get to them.

■ Poisons ■

Keep all chemicals and medicines locked and out of your children's reach. Period. Just doing this one simple thing will prevent most accidental poisonings.

After you've done that, here are other suggestions for safeguarding your children against accidental poisonings:

- Keep all products in their original packages. It's all too common to pour paint or turpentine into a milk jug for storage, but to your child it looks like something good to drink. Another reason for keeping the original container is that you'll be able to inform the poison control center about the ingredients if your child ingests a poison.
- Many pediatricians think that vitamins shaped like cartoon figures encourage children to take pills. There's some truth to this. Children should not think that medicines are candy. Also, be aware that children can overdose on vitamins with iron.
- Make sure all medicine bottles have childproof lids, and put the lids back on every time you open the bottle.
- Never leave pills or open bottles of medicine on a bathroom sink, even for a few minutes.
- If you must store medicines in the refrigerator, make sure they are kept in containers with childproof lids and hide them in the back.
- Always read the labels for exact dosage. If you have any doubt, call your doctor or pharmacist.
- Empty containers from dangerous products should never be used as toys. They might contain a little bit of hazardous material, and they also confuse the child about what an appropriate plaything looks like. If this empty container is OK to play with, why not one that's full?
- Tobacco is poisonous. Keep all cigarettes and other tobacco products away from children.
- Teach your children about the dangers of medicines and household chemicals.

The High Chair

The biggest danger from high chairs is that children who aren't strapped in or not closely supervised fall out and injure themselves. Never count on the tray to keep the child in the chair. **Always use the strap that holds the child at the waist and between the legs.** Be sure the locking mechanism for the legs is locked at all times. Never allow a child to stand in the chair.

SAFETY BY THE NUMBERS

Falls are the leading cause of unintentional injury to infants under age one who are treated in emergency rooms.

Keep the chair away from walls so the child can't push against it and knock over herself and the chair. Don't let older children hang on to the chair. They can tip it over.

The Bathroom

Bathroom dangers revolve around water. Check the temperature of your water to make sure it's not scalding hot. Many parents change the water heater's thermostat so it does not exceed 120 degrees Fahrenheit. The old elbow-in-the-water test is perfect for checking water temperature.

SAFETY BY THE NUMBERS

Drownings are the leading cause of accidental death in Florida for children under five years old.

Follow these additional suggestions to childproof your bathroom:

- Turn off the faucet handles tightly to prevent your child from turning them on.
- Never leave an infant alone in the tub.
- Rugs with nonskid mats will help prevent slips and trips when you're carrying the baby.
- In addition to keeping all medicines in a locked cabinet, keep shampoos, deodorants, and other personal-care products safely stowed too. Many are poisonous.

- Keep all toilet lids down. While some children have fallen into toilets and drowned, it's more common for mischievous children to throw paper and towels down and try to flush it. Either way, keep the toilet off-limits, even if it means using a lock.
- Don't leave toilet-bowl cleaners or disinfectants on the floor.
- Unplug all electrical appliances and store them away.
- Remove the lock from the bathroom door so you'll have a way in if your child tries to lock himself in (and you know he will.)
- Consider using plastic drinking cups instead of glasses for the bathroom. In fact, don't allow any glass items in the bathroom. Replace the glass in your shower with plastic or safety glass.

The Nursery

More infants are injured and die from accidents involving cribs than any other nursery item. Fortunately for babies, cribs now being sold by retailers in the United States must meet Consumer Products Safety Commission standards for safety. However, these standards only became law in 1974 (they've been updated and expanded since), and many cribs are still being sold that were built before the law took effect. In addition, while the crib itself may meet standards for safety, items in and around the crib are often responsible for injuring children.

SAFETY BY THE NUMBERS

Nursery-room equipment was responsible for ninety-two thousand emergency room visits in 1989.

If you're buying a second-hand crib or if you're using an old one, check the following points to make sure it's safe for your baby:

- Decorative cutouts between the corner post and robe rails—the tops of the end panels—may trap a child's head. Look for a crib design without cutouts or one where the opening between the post and the rail is too small to trap the child's head.

- Corner posts should not extend more than one-sixteenth inch above the end panel. They are catching points for necklaces or cords around the neck. Saw them off, and sand smoothly if necessary.
- Never use a crib that has missing slats. The distance between slats should never be more than 2 3/8 inches.
- Mattresses should fit snugly. You should not be able to stick two fingers between the mattress edge and the side of the crib. A child can easily get his head caught in that small of a space.
- Most crib accidents occur when babies climb out and fall on the floor. Use a crib with as large a distance between the top of the side rail and the mattress as you can find. You should also cut down on the number of large stuffed toys and pillows in the crib because children will use them to stand on.
- If the crib was manufactured before 1978, it could have lead paint on it. (Laws limiting lead in paint went into effect in February 1978.) Have the paint removed by someone who knows how to do it safely. If you repaint the crib yourself, use new household enamel, not old paint that may contain lead.

Aside from the crib itself, you should follow these crib-related safety hints:
- Keep the crib away from drapery and window-blind cords. Never hang any string or cord from a crib.
- Always raise and lock the side rails as soon as your child can stand up. When the child is thirty-five inches tall, he or she should probably forgo the crib and sleep in a bed. If the child is too immature for a bed, you can buy mesh side panels to keep him or her from rolling off.
- Never use thin plastic such as trash bags or dry-cleaning bags as mattress covers. They can stick to a child's face and cause suffocation.
- Check the crib's hardware, especially the mattress-support hangers, for tightness. Screws can work lose over time.

- Any toy, mobile, or visual-stimulation object should be securely tied at both ends of the crib so it will not fall into the crib. When your child begins to push up on his or her hands and knees, remove all of these items.
- Keep all lotions and powders away from the crib and out of the baby's reach.

The Living Room

The main toddler hazard in the living room is sharp-edged furniture. Although you will soon realize you can't protect your baby from getting hurt when he or she flops—falling down is part of the learning process—you can minimize the pain and prevent severe injury.

Glass-topped tables are particularly dangerous to new walkers, so you should either cover the edges with soft mate-

---

■ Harmful Plants ■

Many household and garden plants are harmful if eaten. The following list doesn't include all toxic garden and houseplants, only the most popular ones. The names given are those most commonly used, although the plant may have different common names in different areas. That's why the Latin name is also given.

Before you place any plant in your home or garden check with your local poison control center about its potential for harm. Also, keep all flower bulbs and seeds away from children.

Lily of the valley (*Convallaria majalis*)
Chokeberry (*Prunus virginiana*)
Daphne (*Daphne mezereum*)
Elephant ear (dieffenbachia)
Rhubarb (*Rheum rhabarbarum*)
Japanese yew (Taxus cuspidata)
Wisteria (*wisteria*)
Jack-in-the-pulpit (*Arisaema triphyllum*)
Deadly nightshade (*Atropa belladonna*)
Rhododendron (*Rhododendron*)
American ivy (*Parthenocissus quinquefolia*)

rial or remove them from the room. Another danger is fireplace tools; a baby can fall on a poker and receive a serious injury. As the baby gets older and the danger of falling on fireplace tools becomes lessened, these items become "weapons" in the hands of toddlers. Fireplace tools are not only filthy but are heavy enough to smash things. They should be stored away and not brought out until needed.

Make sure your fireplace has a secure screen, and be sure to keep all matches out of the baby's reach.

Ashtrays should be empty—tobacco and filters are poisonous. Never leave a lighted cigarette in the ashtray when the baby is around.

In the dining room, store away the tablecloth for a while; babies love to tug on them. Keep chafing dishes in the center of the table, and be very careful when using candles.

Basements and Work Areas

These areas contain so many dangers for babies (adults, too) that you might want to keep it off-limits until baby matures. It's just too difficult, if not impossible, to babyproof work areas, and a gate in the doorway might be a good way to keep baby away. A locked door is even better.

Gates

When choosing a baby gate, pick one that isn't the *accordion-style*. These have diamond-shaped areas that can trap babies' necks and strangle them, although an accordion-style might be okay if the diamond-shaped openings are very small—no more than 1 1/2 inches in width—to prevent head entrapment. A better choice is a straight-topped gate with rigid mesh screen.

Be sure the gate is securely anchored in the doorway or against the walls. Children have been known to push the gates open. If you're using the kind of gate that holds by pushing against the doorway, make sure the expanding pressure bar is on the side away from the baby. Children have used this bar for a toehold to climb over the gate.

Electrical Outlets

Children can't injure themselves just by playing around electrical outlets. The problem arises when they start to explore the outlet slots with metal items such as keys. Putting plastic plug covers into the outlets may help (with the emphasis on the word *may*). Many children can easily extract these plastic plugs. A better choice is a spring-loaded cover of some sort that snaps closed and covers the outlet when an appliance isn't plugged in. Permanent screw-on covers are fine for outlets that you don't use but inconvenient if you need the outlet often.

Again, while these outlet covers will protect your child from harm, nothing can replace discipline and teaching the child not to stick things in the outlets.

Suffocation

Suffocation is the second leading cause of household deaths among children one to four years old. Statisticians divide this suffocation into two causes. The first is suffocation by ingesting a tiny object such as a small toy or ball or even food, and the second is smothering by things like bedclothes and plastic bags.

These two hazards, like many other childhood dangers, can often be prevented. The next two sections discussing toys and food will show you how.

Toys and Other Objects

All toys have age suggestions on the box, saying something like, "for children three and up" or "not recommended for children under one year old." These are not just recommendations based on a child's skill or enjoyment level, they are often based on the possibility that the child might swallow the entire object or that the toy is composed of parts the child might remove and then swallow. **Pay attention to age recommendations on toys.** They could save your child's live.

The Consumer Product Safety Commission (CPSC) has the responsibility for setting mandatory toy-safety regulations and writing the age suggestions. For the most part, the agency has done a good job of weeding out harmful products. However, it's still up to parents to protect their children from unsafe toys. For one thing, the CPSC may not know there's a problem with a toy until children have been injured or killed. At that time, a recall is initiated.

In addition, be mindful that toys that are safe and suitable for older children may find their way to younger children for whom the toy could be dangerous. For example, five-year-olds love balloons and play with them all the time, but in the hands of an infant an uninflated or burst balloon can be dangerous if swallowed. **More children have suffocated from uninflated balloons or pieces of balloons than any other type of toy.**

While we're discussing suffocation hazards, let's also talk about other dangers from toys. To discuss every toy and its hazards would be impossible, but the suggestions that follow are general guidelines for choosing safe toys for your children. Remember, follow the age recommendations on the toys themselves. They supply some of the best information you can find. Of course, all children are different. Some children learn earlier than others the dangers of putting toys in their mouths.

Let's start with a basic safety idea: **the smaller the child the larger the toy.** Infant toys such as rattles, teethers, and squeeze animals should be large enough so they cannot enter the baby's throat. If the toy isn't one continuous piece make sure it holds together well. Test it yourself and see if you can break it. (Well, sure you can break it if you really try, but give it a reasonable test to ensure that it's not easily broken.)

There is an exception to the big-toy rule. Newborns can be smothered by large stuffed animals if they can't turn over yet and the toy is on their face. Likewise, newborns should sleep on their sides, propped by a folded blanket, or on their backs until they get a little older. No pillows or stuffed animals in the crib, please, until the child can turn over and move around a bit.

Check all toys periodically for damage or wear. A toy that was safe when new may be have loose parts your child can swallow after it's been used. When wooden toys become worn they can expose splinters, nails, or screws.

Keep older children's toys away from younger children. Teach older children about the hazards of sharing toys with their younger siblings. All toys should be put away when not used. This also will help keep inappropriate toys out of youngsters' hands. Check all hand-me-down toys for safety. Explain to children how to use toys properly.

■ Mandatory Government Regulations ■ for Toys

For all ages
- There should be no shock or thermal hazards in electrical toys.
- There should be no toxic materials in toys.
- Lead amounts should be severely limited in toys.

For children under three years old
- Toys should be unbreakable, able to withstand abuse.
- Toys should have no small parts or pieces that could become lodged in the throat. The toys themselves must be strong enough not to separate into small pieces.

Under Eight Years Old
- No electrical toys should have heating elements.
- Toys should have no sharp points.
- Toys should have no sharp edges.

Toy chests can be dangerous. Many injuries and some deaths have occurred because toy-chest lids have fallen on children. Make sure the lid has a hinge that allows it to stay up in any position. If your toy chest doesn't have that feature, replace it with one that does or remove the lid entirely. Some people suggest that toy chests have air holes just in case your child decides to play "cave" inside the box. Check the toy chest for sharp edges or hinges.

Avoid toys that shoot objects that can injure eyes.

Avoid toys with long strings or cords for infants and young children. Never hang toys with long strings, loops, or ribbons in cribs where children can become strangled. Crib arches and other activity toys are great for infants lying on their backs, but remove them from the crib when the child can get up and reach them.

By regulation, all toys with sharp objects are prohibited, but older toys not covered by the regulation may still be around and worn toys can sometimes eventually show sharp edges.

As your child gets older, he or she will want to play with more and more sophisticated toys that require parental attention and supervision; this is especially true for toys that are mechanical or electrical in nature.

Be careful with toys such as cap pistols that make loud noises. Children should be instructed never to use them inside the house and never to fire them near their ears.

Electric toys should always be battery operated, not plugged into the wall, until your child is at least eight years old. Electrical toys can not only shock but also burn, and children using electrical toys—plugged into the wall—require adult supervision and instruction.

Food

Nothing is more frightening than seeing your baby choke on food.

While children are learning how to eat solid food they're at a disadvantage: Their throats are still small, they don't have the chewing skills (and maybe not the teeth) to chew thoroughly, and they don't yet know the dangers of cramming as much food as they can into their mouths. For them, it's just plain fun.

As a parent, you should be wary of certain "choking" foods such as hot dogs, nuts, raisins, carrots, and fruits with skin. There are other "dangerous" foods as well, and you should ask your pediatrician about phasing in these choices.

Children just starting to eat can choke on lots of foods, even soft ones. **Above all, learn what to do when your child chokes.** The Heimlich maneuver, for example, is accepted as an excellent method to prevent food suffocation in both children and adults.

Walkers

Walkers have been getting a bad reputation lately with some pediatricians calling for their outright ban. Unfortunately this reputation is deserved: The CPSC estimated that in one year more than twenty-thousand people received emergency room treatment for injuries associated with walkers.

The greatest danger from walkers is from tipping over. They tip when the child leans over to pick something up or when he or she moves from hard flooring to carpeted areas. Also, **falling down stairs is all too common with walkers.** And older walkers with x-frames that look and act like scissors have cut and amputated fingers.

Many pediatricians say that the developmental benefits of walkers are not that great compared with the risks. If you disagree and still want to use a walker, follow these recommendations:

- **Walkers should never be used as babysitters.** Always watch children in walkers. * Use walkers only on smooth floors. Carpet edges and steps are dangerous.
- Always use gates at the top of the stairs.
- Make sure the walker doesn't have sharp edges or points and that x-joints are covered to keep baby's fingers out of the area.

Other Baby Items

Every time you turn around, it seems that someone has invented a new device to carry or transport your baby. These are great conveniences, but they require some care to be safe.

Backpacks

Proper fit is the key to safety. Your baby must fit well into the pouch and the leg openings must be small enough so he or she won't fall through.

Use all the straps, especially the shoulder restraints that keep the baby from rising up and out of the backpack. Don't forget the baby is on your back when you're walking under low trees and in doorways. And when you stoop, bend at the knees, not at the waist. It's not only the proper way to bend and keep from straining your back, but it will keep the baby from going headfirst out of the backpack.

Hook-On Chairs

Friction keeps hook-on seats snug against the table. When using one, make sure the frame itself is locked securely and that both rubber "stops" on the top and the underneath are pushed tightly against the table. It's not a bad idea to place a regular chair underneath the hook-on seat in case it should unhook.

Make sure your baby is restrained by the straps, and never leave a child unattended.

Carrier Seats

The CPSC estimates that thousands of children each year are taken to emergency rooms because of injuries sustained by carrier seats. Most of the injuries are from children falling out of the seat or from the seat and baby falling together.

Buy a carrier seat that has a wide, sturdy base, and always use the restraining straps. Never place the carrier seat on a table or chair unless you're sitting next to it. An active baby can move these seats easily and quickly, especially if the seat has plastic feet that can be slippery.

Carrier seats are not car seats and offer no protection while riding in a car.

Pacifiers

All pacifiers sold in the United States must meet government safety regulations. They must be strong enough not to come apart. The shields must be large enough to make it difficult for the baby to get it in his or her mouth, but the shields must also have holes for the baby to breathe through if that does happen.

Pacifiers may not be sold with strings. Each pacifier must also carry the following warning:

"Warning: Do not tie pacifier around child's neck as it presents a strangulation danger."

A short ribbon can be attached to the pacifier and clipped to the baby's shirt if you'd like, but make sure there are no loops that can get around the baby's neck. If the pacifier were to get caught on something, the clip would simply unsnap.

Because they're rubber, pacifiers can deteriorate with use. Throw them out if you notice any deterioration.

Strollers

More than ten thousand children in an average year are injured enough to require emergency-room treatment for stroller-related incidents. The main cause: children falling out. The main cure: Always use the seat belt, and never leave your child in the stroller unattended. Simple, eh?

When buying a stroller, consider your child's size. If your child is too tall, he or she could lean over the side or back and topple the stroller. Each stroller should have working brakes. Never hang anything heavy from the handles. It can cause the stroller to tip backward. When folding or unfolding the stroller, keep children away so they don't get their fingers stuck. Watch your own fingers too.

Car Seats

Traffic accidents claim more children's lives than any other cause.

Before purchasing a car seat, read your car owner's

manual. It will give you specific instructions about using car seats in concert with the seat belts. In some cars, you need an extra locking clip (they often come with the car seat) to hold the car seat securely. Also make sure the car seat fits on your car's seat. At least 80 percent of the car seat's base should rest on your car's seat.

SAFETY BY THE NUMBERS

Motor-vehicle crashes are the leading cause of accidental deaths in infants under one year old; the next most common causes are drowning and fire or burns.

Select a car seat that's easy to use, because the easier it is to use, the more inclined you'll be to use it. If you have more than one car in the family, it's a good idea to buy the type of car seat (usually for infants) that fits into a base which is then strapped into the car. By placing a base in each car, life becomes a lot easier because you don't have to keep switching car seats and bases between cars. When you take the car seat out, it becomes a baby carrier. The handles often swing down, providing a sturdy base on which the carrier can rest outside the car.

Follow the instructions that come with the car seat. It's been shown that three out of four car seats are installed incorrectly. Don't assume that the car seat is securely fastened just because you've gotten the seat belts through the car seat's body. Pull forward and side to side on the car seat to make sure it doesn't move. Also make sure the child's restraining straps are snug. Again, follow the instruction manual precisely for maximum protection.

Be very careful if you're buying a used car seat. Those manufactured before January 1, 1981, the day government regulations took effect, may not be crashworthy. Check the fittings for rust and the belts for deterioration, and don't buy a used car seat unless the owner has the instruction manual. Never buy a used car seat that has been involved in an accident. Check to see if a car seat has been recalled by consulting the National Highway Traffic Safety Administration's recall report. (Call the auto safety hot line: 800–424-9393.)

For new car seats, always fill out and return the warranty card. This will allow the manufacturer to contact you if a safety defect is discovered.

Windows

Each spring when we open our windows to let in fresh air, we put our children in peril. One of the saddest accidents is children falling from open windows; this is made all the sadder because it is so easy to prevent.

Don't count on screens to keep children inside. This may be parents' biggest mistake when it comes to window safety. Plastic screens, which comprise most of today's screening material, are easily pushed out by children. Even metal screens, especially if they're old, can rip easily with only moderate force.

If you must leave windows open, put a metal grate or some other child-protection device in front of the window.

Never leave a chair or table in front of windows. This gives children easy access to the window.